A SMALL MEXICAN WORLD

DON PANCHO AND HIS BROTHER

BY WILLIAM SPRATLING

With portraits and decorations by the author

Foreword by Diego Rivera
Introduction by Lesley Byrd Simpson

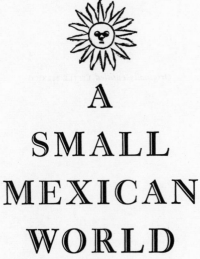

A
SMALL
MEXICAN
WORLD

originally entitled LITTLE MEXICO

LITTLE, BROWN AND COMPANY
Boston • *Toronto*

LIBRARY OF CONGRESS CATALOG CARD NO. 64-22120

Originally entitled LITTLE MEXICO

*Published simultaneously in Canada
by Little, Brown & Company (Canada) Limited*

PRINTED IN THE UNITED STATES OF AMERICA

This little Mexico, a small world in itself, is of the same earth which forms the Mexican's beloved *patria chica* — his original homeland.

A provincial verse reads:

> *Cuando yo muera, comadre,*
> *Haga de mi barro un jarro.*
> *Si tienes sed, de mi bebe,*
> *Y si a tus labios el barro se pega,*
> *Es un beso de tu charro.*

> When I die, my dear,
> Of my clay make a cup.
> When you have thirst, from me drink.
> The clay which clings to your lips
> Is a kiss from your lover.

This, then, is dedicated to life in the provinces, the heart of Mexico.

WILLIAM SPRATLING

Taxco-el-Viejo
April, 1964

CONTENTS

Coyoacan. Saturday, 29th of August of 1931
Sr. Don Guillermo Spratling.

Taxco, Guerrero.

My dear Bill;
I have received the manuscript of your book which you were good enough to let me see. Many thanks.

The publication of this book makes me very happy, you have lived here a long time and for this and other reasons — above all, because you love Mexico and because Mexico loves you — it is your right to make a portrait of that which you know so well. You have made a portrait of Mexico composed of many small portraits of people and things.

Your portraits have the acuteness and grace of those painted by certain masters in my country who died before I was born. Those portraits were made with precision and tenderness and contain irony and love.

Your book is in itself a portrait and in that sense needs no preface; it explains itself.

Your friend, who congratulates you,
Diego Rivera

Coyoacán. Sábado 29 de Agosto de 1931
Señor Don Guillermo Spratling

Taxco. Guerrero.

Mi querido Bill;

He recibido el manuscrito de tu libro
que me hiciste favor de dejarme conocer.
muchas gracias.

Me alegro mucho de la publicación de este
libro tuyo, tienes mucho tiempo de vivir aquí.
y por esto y otras razones — sobre todo que quieres
a México y México te quiere — tienes derecho de
hacer el retrato de lo que conoces bien.

Has hecho el retrato de México compuesto de
muchos pequeños retratos de gentes y de cosas.

Tus retratos tienen la agudés y el atractivo
de los que pintaban allá en mi tierra algunos
maestros muerto antes de que yo naciera.

Esos retratos están hechos con precisión y ternura
y contienen ironía y amor

Tu libro es un retrato, así. por eso no ne=
cesita prefacio, se presenta solo.

Te felicita tu amigo. Diego Rivera.

Dear Bill:

Having just reread one of my most treasured volumes, which occupies an honored place between Charles Flandrau's Viva Mexico! *and Fanny Calderón's* Life in Mexico, *I wish first off to express my delight at the prospect of seeing* Little Mexico *in print again. What a vivid portrait it is of our* patria chica, *and what a host of memories it brings tumbling into my mind!*

In the summer of 1931, when I had not even heard of Bill Spratling, a friend at the American Embassy invited me to spend a weekend in the Morrow House at Cuernavaca. I was completely charmed by its warmth and grace, and heard that a young architect named William Spratling had restored it. (Actually, you had made the illustrations for a book about it, but no matter.) I decided I should have to know him.

The opportunity soon came. Brownie Aguirre took me to Taxco and put me up in the house you had built for Moisés Saenz. There I inevitably met Natalie Scott, the grande dame *of Taxco, with whom I fell in love, as did everyone who knew her. Natalie, who had a passion for taking care of lost gringos, had me up to her funny little house perched on the edge of a barranca. While we were having tea and habanero (a gruesome combination), we were interrupted by a barking of dogs and a clumping of boots, and a character in blue jeans, followed by his dogs, strode across the veranda. He greeted Natalie briefly, dismissed me with a glance, and walked off. I must have looked puzzled, for Natalie said: "Oh, don't mind him. It's only Bill. He thinks you're a tourist. I'll fix it up." Which she did that afternoon at Doña Berta's Bar, where, over several glasses of Doña Berta's best, I made the great breakthrough.*

It was a happy beginning of a memorable year. Shoals of refugees, fleeing the Great Depression, were coming to Mexico, the new Land of Promise, advertised by Stuart Chase, in his Mexico: A Study of the Two Americas, *as a country that had solved the problem of living with itself. Painters, writers, and scholars swarmed in to breathe the invigorating air. They gathered around the towering figure of Diego Rivera and soaked up his startling mixture of Karl Marx and nonsense, along with his vastly stimulating ideas about what could be done with an art deriving from the rich heritage of aboriginal Mexico. They collected in bars and studios, and talked endlessly. It was an intoxicating and delightful interval, described many years later by Carleton Beals, in* A House in Mexico. *Hart Crane was nursing a hopeless plan to write an epic poem on the Conquest, and drowning his frustrations in tequila, while Peggy Baird and Mary Doherty undertook the equally hopeless task of domesticating him. Paca Toor, an old Mexican hand, was publishing her* Mexican Folkways, *at the same time holding a kind of salon at the top of a crazy apartment building on Abraham González resembling the Leaning Tower of Pisa, which one ascended by an elevator like an inclined plane railway. The floors slanted correspondingly, and one rather expected the ricketty structure to collapse when Diego's immense bulk slid to the lower end of the room. At Paca's place and Emily Edwards's studio one met a whole constellation of celebrities: Carlos Mérida, Jean Charlot, Miguel Covarrubias, David Siqueiros, Rufino Tamayo, María Izquierdo, René d'Harnoncourt, and Juan O'Gorman. I don't remember seeing you there, for you rarely came to the city in those days, being fully occupied with your dream of reviving the ancient art of the silversmiths in Taxco. Tamayo and Angel Salas were easily persuaded to play and sing the shocking ballads of the Revolution, which had to compete with the roar of conversation. Our dear Marian [Simpson] joined us at the middle of that year and gathered impressions that have lasted to this day and enriched her own painting.*

We were all writing, or intending to write; painting, or intending to paint. A good many really did. Hart Crane, after his year of agony, completed his last great poem, The Broken Tower, *and died.*

Then, one day in the spring of 1932, while I was strolling down Madero, you clutched me by the arm and steered me into a bookshop. "This caballero," you said to the clerk, "wants to buy a copy of Little Mexico!" Which I did, whereupon we repaired to Bach's Bar to celebrate. And then came the heart-breaking word: Cape and Smith, the publishers, had dissolved their partnership, and Little Mexico was left an orphan. I forget where we sought comfort, but I think it was at Doña Berta's in Taxco.

This was sad, for I now loved the book and the Mexico it pictured: the lovely, cruel, simple (perhaps not so simple) life of remote villages lost in the mountains of the south. The story of your voyage down the Balsas, admirably illustrated with your sensitive and vigorous drawings, is unforgettable. For it, and for your many kindnesses to me, I shall always be in your debt.

And now Little Mexico is to be born again! This is excellent news and will be welcomed by every lover of Mexico. Where shall the christening be, my dear Bill? I suggest the Rancho Spratling, and soon!

Con todo afecto,

Lesley Byrd Simpson

A SMALL MEXICAN WORLD

I
PLACE

The little cantina *has coloured paper cutouts —
not advertising — across a big mirror obscured with
fly spots and other minor casualties. Outside it is
dark and the cobbles of the Calle del Arco are shiny
in the wet. The church is faintly luminous in the re-
flected light from the silly kiosk in the garden. The
bells are ringing for evening mass or perhaps a baptism, and a few Indian women, barefoot, almost
theatrical in the uniform folds of their sad rebozos,
pass the door on their way.*

*Blas is a little tight and talkative. So are the two
Americans who sell blasting supplies. They are playing dominoes at the other table.*

We are talking about history. Imagine, says Blas,

how it was twenty years ago! Hardly an Indian in the plaza spoke a word of English. Even now when I go to Tepecuacuilco to buy ajonjolí and other grains, imagine how it would be if, when the girl tells me " Macuili," I did not understand and couldn't ask her if it did not affect her conscience to charge so dearly! De veras, Señor, one has to speak Mexicano! It is sometimes necessary in order to eat! At the other table, one of the Americanos is explaining Mexico to his partner.

. . . you see, first there were these pyramids, but Moctezuma was a kind of a sissy and he let the Spaniards capture 'em. Then Cortés — he was a Spaniard — and Maximilian had a revolution and Maximilian he won — I ain't quite sure whether it was Maximilian or this guy Díaz which won, but it was the first revolution. It was at Cholula, and I read somewhere it was awful bloody. Then Villa come along, and then they had another revolution. . . . This time Calles, he won. . . . And then, finally, there was the Religious Question. This society called the Goodwillers settled that, though some say Morrow he had a hand in it. . . . These birds ain't got nothing to kick about!

THE TOWN

THE houses of the town are shining and compact, a study in red and white and green. The poverty and simplicity of it goes all unsuspected. Each house, resolving the problem of an odd corner, the sudden declivity of a *barranca* or a spur of virgin rock, has resulted individually. Yet the whole has that same unity of growth which exists in plants. For this reason people like to refer to it as " picturesque," as an " elegant example of the colonial," " ravishing," and so on. Two thirds of its houses are of unplastered adobe or palm-thatched *jacal*. But it is difficult to see these for the church. They melt into the rocky wilderness above and below the town.

Seen from above, the highway through town, the

5

camino real, is a twisted vine, with tendrils. In the centre, with the thick trees of the plaza forming a single green circlet at its base, blooms the architectural brilliance of the church for a flower. It is a product of the inefficiently integrated colonization of short-sighted Spanish colonials and it long since ceased to be expressive of life here.

The people of this town have had power and money, or some of them had. They have been exploited, exiled, brought back to new possibilities. Potentialities do remain. Here was the first source of precious metal for the conquerors in New Spain. Its hills are still thickly veined with silver and the wild mountains of this region are the richest part of a vast uncharted mine called the state of Guerrero. The paradox is that neither the Mexicans nor the foreigners ever did much more than continue the earliest diggings, in the same way that they never did anything toward developing the vast regions of Mexico which lay in the hot country, and the town is still poor and in place of accumulated wealth there are now only perpetually hopeful old men. Circumstances have intervened.

The old gentleman who brings charcoal in the late afternoon shows me samples of ore. So does the white-bearded old Marcelino Alemán when I go to see him about his idols. Casually I ask, more for the sake of his interest than mine, where the samples are from. Over there! — over there! with a wave of a withered old paw toward the mountains. He has had them so long that he is vague as to sources. But he has not lost faith in an Ultimate Abundance. Blas Vela, my companion on various minor explorations, has gold mines in Tlaxmaloc. The wall of the gallery above his humble garden is filled with crystal bits that show silver, of rust-red rocks that glint with gold and there are even a few geometric, pale amethysts.

On my balcony are samples of ore placed alongside the conch and the potted geraniums. The postmaster uses them for paperweights. Children play store with ore specimens from their father's table. . . .

One begins to think of the town itself as a sample of mineralized Mexico — its history a collection of shining veins running through the grey of an ungenerous past.

There is something complete and self-contained about the place. For a long time, during a period of inaccessibility and lack of means for working mines, it was literally forgotten — even by Mexico City. That could easily happen again without any more serious results than before. Their problems remain the same. World economic depressions mean little here and if the exchange goes sky high — it has little to do with them, who deal in centavos. The men, the older ones, live in the future of their mines, awaiting the day when good living will again be universal and one can drink French wine instead of Taxco water. They are quite innocent of Mr. Chase's Machine Age — even though the business of becoming a mechanic fascinates most of the young *pelados* who hang about the plaza.

The lives of the women here are the same as the lives of women in every other small town in Mexico. Marriage, for the poor, is nothing to worry about. Women bear children regardless. The part of their lives which is not absorbed in bearing children, in keeping the straw mats rolled in the daytime and unfurled at night, in keeping the pot boiling and the corn prepared for the day's *tortillas,* is given rhetorically and completely to the church. Young, they are frequently beautiful; but they become old suddenly. The events of a faintly luminous electric light system and a motor-driven mill for making their corn into *masa,* have had little effect on their daily life. Fashions, movies, time-saving devices mean almost nothing.

When José de la Borda came here in 1717 what might this town have been like? Probably it was a much smaller and more purely Indian village, economically self-sufficient. They would have used their precious metals solely for adornment. Perhaps it was no more than a *cuadrilla,* as they call those villages of four or five families which have their houses on as many hills.

Borda used only the name of the town he found,

V. R. del Sor D. Jose
de la BORDA natural de
los Reynos de Francia de o-
cindo en este Rl. siendo de di-
et y seis años de edad y para
sostenerse con   tomo dg
ro de la Minería, en el que hizo la
fama, y con liberalidad
construto este suntuoso
Templo. A su solicitud se le conce-
dte con innumerables Indulgens
lo adorno de Vaso Sagrados y
Ricas Vestiduras   Pano eterno
Monumento de Gratitud se
coloco en esta Sala Capi-
bular, despues de sus di-
as; por que su mucha
umildad no consinti-
o se colocase qu-
ando vivio

Dibujo fielmente.
tomado por Guillermo Spratling del
retrato original que se encuentra en
lo Parroquia de Taxco-de-Alarcon

and, in the accumulated power and riches of his un-
tiring exploitation, built this. He did it well. It would
take a vigorous nature and one more uncompromis-
ing than that of the native Indian to conceive a city
on these tortuous slopes. Not only was the town
built to the order of Borda, but the wild and desert
wastes of Guerrero were pierced with hundreds of
kilometres of laboriously cobbled roads with walls.
All that to produce wealth for one energetic and
domineering little foreigner. Mexico's single function in those days was to serve as a source for such
fortunes. Even the church claimed the right to ac-
cumulate. . . . Borda feared God and the Church,
and he placated the Virgin with lovely structures of
pink stone and azure tiles. Therefore, this town.

As I sit in the plaza in the late afternoons the
scene varies only in details. The little stands and the
line of old women who sit on the cobbles, baskets in
laps, selling hot tortillas or tamales, enjoy the same
little flurry of trade which occurs daily about six.
. . . Some miners have come in from Pichagua and
Santa Rosa. They stroll around the plaza looking
for recognition from the girls as they pass in the
opposite direction. This business of " taking a turn "
is ritual in Mexico and an indispensable social function. You see all the world go by at this hour. You
enjoy the fresh evening air, and, meeting your
friends, are regaled with complete details of a " Personal " column in a non-existent local press. For

young girls especially it is a titillating and delectable process. Mothers meet and compare babies. Fathers sit or stroll under the great trees and discuss whether or not the Americans and the Spaniards are going to invest in the mines — of how badly investment is wanted or not wanted (Mexican capital, being an unknown quantity, is never mentioned) and when the federal tax collector is going to ask the municipal president to close the house called number fifteen. . . . Elio, young Pineda, and I watch a dog fight and plan to go to a pool called the Big Dive to swim in the morning. . . . There is Miguel Maldito, ex-bandit, who now runs a truck, the tall Indian in his shirt sleeves over there, complimenting a señora on her baby (similar to the one he or the municipal president was admiring at this time yesterday). Two flirtatious young things from the next town are waiting for him to buy them an ice-cream *paleta*. . . . Children, chasing each other in the gathering dust, like young goats, butt each other between your legs, scream and fly off in an ecstasy of play that is a part of the gregarious instinct. . . . Just at the corner, their chairs placed on the cobbles outside the old doctor's apothecary shop, sit five or six old men. The younger generation refers to them as the *coloniales,* because they have no greater delight than to show distinguished visitors, usually American school-teachers and goodwillers, the colonial glories of the town. Every evening they are gathered there, gossiping and making Mexican jokes about burros and women. There you will find old Doctor Antonino — who was a Zapatista, Don Margarito, once *jefe político* of the town under Díaz, the Sacristan of the Parroquia, and another old fellow, once rich, who sells postcards to the tourists when any such happen to pass and who will sell them mines if they let him. Sometimes, Felipe — whose father was head of the garrison here under Huerta and was later exiled to Cuba by Don Margarito's Zapatistas — and I sit in with the coloniales for a cigarette and a little reminiscent conversation. . . . A few doors down the street are some fellows who keep a combination pressing-tailor-barber-shop. Every evening one of them, the same boy who plays the bass viol in the band, gets out a guitar about this time. They sing *Las Mañanitas, Coni, Coni,* and so on, while friends sit there against the wall in the dark, or in the light of a rising moon, and think of Luisa or Jovita, or perhaps of a glorious bullfight they saw last week in Iguala. Sometimes they even sing the slightly bawdy *Palo Verde,* or *La Cucaracha,* the same version Pancho Villa used to sing. Then you can hear ripples of laughter in the other places up and down the street.

Signs of the zodiac, heroic bulls, stars and other favourite insignia are wrought in a mosaic of black basalt in the cobbles of the camino real. It is in the

CAMINO REAL

best tradition of local workers in stone. Such details are taken for granted by the people who live here. As a matter of fact they are only clearly visible after the first washing rains of the wet season. It was along this road, embroidered with the same fantastic signs, that for a long time only burro trains with silver, and an occasional diligence coach passed. Later, armies and leaders of the Independence came through. Porfirio Díaz and his friends entered by this road — entered with their revolution, promising they would not conscript the young men from here, which is what they immediately did. Zapata and his cavalry dashed through this street, changing the course of the town's history overnight and ending inanely its first breath of prosperity in a hundred years. The same thing happened to hundreds of other Mexican towns. . . . Today all these elements must live together. And they do, because all revolutions are not necessarily effective, even though they appear so at the moment. And because all good revolutionists cannot go to Paris. . . . Now occasional automobiles rush through, or stop for a bottle of beer and some postcards, on their way down to Iguala and the coast. But muleteers, their burro trains laden with charcoal, timber, and shipments of rich ore, still troop through the town by the camino real.

Its windings follow the vast corrugations of the barrancas, spanning ravines where necessary with good colonial bridges. From the mosaic star and circle of the Plazuela Abasolo the road takes one narrow sweep upward to the Plaza Borda — the *zócalo* as it is more properly called in every good Mexican village — there is a detour of the green-black shadows of the Plaza and the pink flash of the church, then the camino glides on toward the Plaza Hidalgo, past a bad cement figure of the father of Mexican Independence, then out by the chapel of the Virgen de la Luz, and downward to Tierra Caliente and Iguala, three thousand feet below.

In this direction, toward the Pacific, the hills are like creased velvet. There lie Tlamacuzapa and Juliantla toward the Cerro Azul; Teloloapan is over there, beyond that farthest range, which is known to be only black rock and cactus clothed in intolerable heat.

One can refer to almost everything below the town as of Tierra Caliente. But for the vast mountain regions above, rugged, impregnable, of no economic use except for a remote mine or two, there is not even a name. It was into these regions that the tribes fled from the early Spaniards. If they were not pursued it was because they had nothing the conquerors cared for. The Indians carried with them a few idols and their simple homely arts and for the most part they have remained there apart, out of all contact with Western civilization and entirely innocent of modern exigencies.

True, they come down from time to time to the plaza to trade. But the things they bring are hardly more numerous than the articles which were prime necessities with them before the conquest. Even the names for these domestic utilities remain pure Aztec. The *metate* is the universal instrument for preparing tortillas, as is also the *metlapil,* both sculptured in

stone; the *tepeztate* is the name of the dish into which the ground corn falls; the *comal* is the big clay disk on which the tortillas are baked. All these things they make and sell or trade among themselves. In each village they make one thing, and the village is known for that particular *oficio.*

The ancestors of these people were Aztecs — and the precursors of the Aztecs. There is no one — not

even among the elegant Generals of the Capital or
the theatrical Charros — more " Mexican " than
they are. But they are humble, and unlearned. The
people of the towns, the small shopkeepers, the *mes-
tizos,* like to refer to them as the " Mexicanitos " —
the Little Mexicans.

On the days when there is a market — in this
town it is on Sunday — the Little Mexicans come
in from all the remote places, moving without violence, with their families and burros. With them arrive at the market black stone metates and *molcajetes*
from Piedras Niegras, sombreros and *petates* from
Tlamacuzapa and Huahuastla, herbs and bananas
and coffee from Cacalotenango, *sarapes* from Coate-
pec Harinas, and a thousand other important or desirable commodities. Some come to pay tribute to the
Virgen de la Luz, others to christen a baby or to buy
a coffin pasted with flowered wall-paper. They come
to town in pink undershirts and freshly starched
white *calzones*. Sometimes the pink is more lavender,
with pleated full white waists and a broad silk scarf,
pink or magenta, around a neck that is a golden
brown. Their faces have the same sculptured im-
mutability as the stone masks of the Aztec priests.

It is almost solemn ritual, the Sunday market here.
The town becomes something more than a mere
conventional, bourgeois village (though all villages
in Mexico are incredibly conventional). It is something besides picturesque. Here a subtle and unsus-

pected relationship between bourgeois and primitive Mexico becomes an actuality. If it is not purely Mexican, it is everything which has happened to that country.

TIERRA CALIENTE

Beyond the capital of Mexico, they say, all is Cuautitlán — small town stuff. It is not true. Because beyond, and below Mexico all is " Tierra Caliente" — the hot country. . . . Here in Mexico one says " Tierra Caliente" as though speaking of another land. And it takes on the quality of another land in people's thoughts. It is a Mexico unknown even to the Mexicans. In the same sense it is the country's physical subconscious. *It is vast .and fecund; forbidding and promising; it is practically unexplored and difficult of access. It is a* tierra *but slightly incorporated in the nation. . . .* Allá en tierra caliente! *. . . yes, there is supposed to be much gold there . . . but it is wild country, and also it is infernally hot . . . they say it is not even populated . . . then too there is the* pinto *. . . what if one goes and comes back with the pinto? . . . only* *imagine such a disease! — a disease which affects and discolours an entire people, and about which practically nothing is known . . . white men have killed themselves from sheer disgust of the thing . . . there isn't even a name for it, only " the Discolour." Through all the region traced by the river Balsas there is pinto; but there is much more besides. There are great sierras; rich valleys. There is gold and silver and petroleum, untouched; sugar, ajonjolí and coffee grow abundantly. There are ancient cities, temples, pyramids — vestiges vastly significant of antique culture and the most ancient races of the continent. In open country and in huts of the poor exist sculptured gods in marble, in jade, in exquisitely wrought clay. . . . It is all pregnant with what has been, and what will be Mexico. . . . Tierra Caliente, seen from the mountains of Guerrero or Oaxaca or Vera Cruz, quivers in a distant blue heat. It appears somehow unreal, fantastically impregnable, like Indo-China, or Africa.*

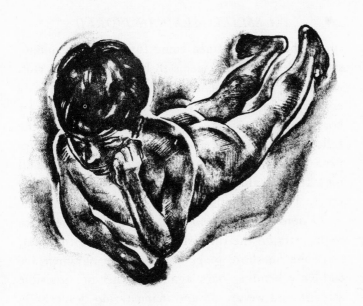

TIERRA CALIENTE

BALSAS. Around a twist in the narrow canyon are grass houses; at their back a churning stream. A spidery-woven bridge of vines paved with twigs stretches its trembling silhouette to the other bank and more grass houses. The mountains have become a gigantic series of perfect cones and pyramids. Suddenly there is the Río Balsas among them. There is a raw, black skeleton of a bridge for the railroad which, crossing here at the end of the line, terminates on the other side with an abrupt gesture, a lone water tank, in the face of wilderness. Tierra Caliente begins here.

It is dark at four in the morning and actually

cool, when the boatmen come for us. A ten minute scramble down what seems to be the face of a cliff, and then, below, silent, formless and mysteriously enveloped in its tent-like covering, is the *pango* or boat which is to take us downstream. One of the fellows has a candle; a woman for whom there happens to be no room is silently weeping, and small pigs are squealing somewhere in the bottom of the craft. The river is invisible.

"*Vamo'*" — "*Vamo' pue'*" — the oarsmen take their seats on the tiny triangular prow of the boat, someone on shore gives a heave, the oarsmen are suddenly bending oars against a rushing, invisible stream, and we are off and manœuvring desperately for the centre of the river, barely avoiding black shadows that are rocks.

Two hours of voyaging thus in the darkness — the people have stowed away wherever they could find space among the cargo. There is hardly a word. There is only a vague movement of oarsmen up forward and the faint creak of the broad leather thongs binding oars to boat and, intermittently, the intensified rush of waters as we enter successive rapids.

At first you see the oarsmen as figures vastly dramatic and detached. It is slave's work, unrelenting. The silhouettes of the two oarsmen and the *mayordomo* sprawled between on lookout suggest something entirely theatrical, as though pre-arranged for dramatic presentation.

I watch these men in the increasing luminousness of early morning light. They are slender, but with broad shoulders. Their skin is dark and polished, with features rather fine, as in Aztec masks — mouths half open and nostrils sharply drawn; spirited and mysterious these faces. Bare feet are planted

on a cross-beam which was the trunk of a small tree. They wear soiled white clothes which are rolled to the knee, with shirts also white, which are open down the front revealing lavender or pink undershirts against bronze skin. And over secret parts, falling as a small black triangle between straining thighs, hangs the *huichol,* or money sack. These things are carried religiously (money or no money) by all male inhabitants of the Balsas. Sometimes the huichol is laughingly referred to as the " sheep."

With the light, people begin to shift positions, to venture a few comments, and to get out oranges and bottles of milk coffee. A lanky, black fellow from the coast tenderly places his charge, a small man-child, on his little rush-bottom chair with a hole in it (obviously made at home), while at the same time he curses the baby for a *cabroncito* of an *esquintle*. Under the feet of the rowers ten little pigs are urgently lunching at their mother's hulk, fastened by the neck to the prow. A kind old gentleman, seated on a folded Iguala hammock (who constantly refers to himself as " the poor doctor "), gets out a green umbrella and a pair of battered opera glasses. Under the stretched canvas toward the rear of this Noah's Ark are the huddled figures of a second shift of oarsmen, sleeping, and some women in blue rebozos, with children, also sleeping. An Indian, a rich farmer (he has a gold tooth), who is seated on a sack of brown sugar at my left, begins to tell me what his village, Tetela-del-Rio, is like. It is the first village we will come to and we should be there now in about five hours.

Meanwhile this wooden box of a boat, shaped a little like a coffin, is moving swiftly down vast gorges where yellow sunlight slants between towering

velvet-blue mountains. The river bed is comparatively narrow and rocky. The pango just misses a
boulder the size of a house and slides aimlessly downward over enormous corrugations of a pale brown
current falling away into rapids.

There is no sign of habitation or of people, until,
rounding a broad turn in the river, we hail the crew
of another boat, strung out waist deep in the water
on the cliff side of the stream, hauling their craft
laboriously, tediously upstream. No greeting, but
the mayordomo of our vessel beats a peculiar tattoo
on the narrow strip of deck where he is sprawled up
forward, answered simply with an "*A-dios*" from
the others. For every day of down-river journeying,
these fellows have from eight to fifteen days of
this backbreaking haul upstream. The mayordomo
informs me that they all begin very young,
in order to accustom themselves to the hardships
of it:

Time passes. We are uncomfortable. The sun
beats down with an amazing directness. A broad
sombrero of palm fibre is good for this. But so far
there are no flies. Flies, says the poor doctor, spread
the pinto. Flies, and sexual intercourse.

A thick covey of green parrots with red feathers
in their wings crosses heavily overhead, with raucous
greetings. There are flocks of white herons and
sometimes a pink one, and an occasional aigrette.
The herons step lengthily and meticulously *en masse*

along the sand bars, giving little attention to the passage of the boat.

The river fascinates. The mountains, instead of flattening, exaggerate their verticality. It gives you the sense of entering a secret country, remote and forgotten; a country not yet realized by civilization.

So the day passes, slowly, but without monotony. The Indians talk almost not at all. This is their country and their life. Monotony does not exist for them. But the old doctor wants to talk politics. It seems he is a Mason. (Mason or Catholic, what difference here?) And he himself initiated a former president of the Republic into the mysteries. There is another from outside, an agrarian, young, very Indian and intelligent, who wants to talk to me about mining here. (To be an American means Unlimited Capital.) He says there is not a gully in all this country where gold cannot be found. But it seems it occurs only in small pockets, or washed down in a fine deposit, as though it were only put there for ornament. A discussion starts at the back of the boat about the next war. It narrows down to the subject of spies. An old fellow with a slightly degenerate, suspicious face holds forth. All the Japanese in this country, for example, are spies! No matter what their occupation may seem to be, they are all spies. They are making intricate maps of the Republic of Mexico. Without a doubt. *Si, Señor!* And the Americans, too. Maybe he suspects me. It develops that

most of the Americans in Mexico, miners, journal-
ists, or what not, are just out gathering information.
What do they plan to do with this country? Why,
the Americans must have it some day, otherwise they
will be conquered by the Asiatics using Mexico as a
base. And as for the Spaniards . . . ! And so on
hasta el ridículo. It turns out that the gentleman
with the slightly degenerate face is a salesman
for German hardware. One of those combination
pioneer-adventurer-salesmen whom one finds ever ac-
tive in the commercial development of countries like
Mexico. His audience is more ingenuous, and more
interesting. Two youngsters. One might be a bull-
fighter. He has that certain air of worldliness which
is found only among the roughnecks of the streets
of the capital, eyes full of cunning and a mouth that
can laugh with real brutality. His companion is
younger, blonder, and appears to be the more credu-
lous. They are very fond of each other and have
many jokes which are private between them. They
never relent in treating the old salesman as an
"uncle," or as an old thing who, they consider,
would give much to be allowed to join in their sport.
. . . A queer group to be travelling in a crude boat
down the Balsas.

Deeply serious discussion, such as the spy question, alternates with broad jokes at the old man, an
occasional firing of pistols at alligators or an eagle,
or gossip about the bull ring and about cronies in

Mexico. The old man confides to me that the boys have been itinerant bull-fighters, that they have turned adventurers on a small scale, and, in short, that they are out for no good; the boys impart rather brutal information about the uncle. They tell me they have fifteen thousand pesos gold with them with which they are going to buy cattle. Later, it seems they are going to Tierra Caliente to buy ajonjolí. At any rate, we all become very good friends.

At Tetela-del-Río there is a tiny inlet where the swift current momentarily eddies in the long face of a cliff. There we land. The Indian with the gold tooth invites us all for a cup of *mezcal,* and for the sake of it we tramp off through the thick underbrush and castor oil plants to the village, which is a mile away up the barranca. Fiery stuff. I buy a little jar of mezcal and carry it back to the crew.

We pass people. This time they are in midstream. It is a man, a woman, and a small boy, swimming. Each stroke takes them a foot or so nearer the opposite bank while the current carries them some yards downstream. The man swims between two big bundles of fire-wood; the woman has a gourd or *balsa* as a float under her right arm (according to the mining fellow this is properly *el Río de las Balsas,* not *el Río Balsas*), and the kid also swims with a balsa. They all are carrying their few rags of

clothing in the deep brims of their sombreros. It is
a comparatively long, straight stretch here. Before
reaching the next curve we can see the three mem-
bers of the family emerge from the brown waters of
the river — a symphony in tones of the same colour.

At Santo Tomás the *agrarista* friend leaves us.
He is going to the gold mines at Temixco. There
are one or two other little places along here. Santa
Rosa, Xochitepec. Before reaching San Miguel Totolapan the mountains become more remote, the
river a little broader, less turbulent, deepening here
in the real Tierra Caliente. Deep golden tones begin to tint the surface of the Balsas. Across the
plains opening southward and westward are the vast
cordilleras of the Sierra Madre. They call it the
Temptation. In that direction from where we now
are the map is marked unexplored. Behind us jagged
peaks, between which we have been moving all this
day, are a metallic blue, dissolving rapidly in gathering dusk. Comelgarto, a silhouette of grass-thatched
huts perched on a bluff, looks like a principal city in
Africa. There are two or three more pangos, the
same as ours, tied there.

It is completely dark on the river. We pass El
Cubo. There is a moon over Temixco, in the direction from which we have come. Downstream another huddle of houses, the silhouette of domes
and a tower on a high bluff indicate San Miguel

Totolapan. That means fried *frijoles* and hot tortillas!

The pueblo of San Miguel Totolapan may seem a little remote and even ragged to the stray outsider, but it is a real centre in Tierra Caliente. We tramp across a rolling plain in the dark, and arrive at a plaza which is actually crowded with people. Flares of pitch pine and little lanterns of tin on poles illu-

minate temporary street shops or eating places. There are tables for gambling at *lotería* in the street, crowded. A dance is solemnly taking place in one corner of an arcade, guitar and the " big pig," the bass viol, assisting. We are the only ones present who are outsiders. Pure Aztec and Tarascan here. It seems that all this is a *fiesta* in order to celebrate the day of San Miguel, patron saint. However, it will be a fifteen-day fiesta.

At a certain little table, one of a whole row of such tables, where the cooking is being done just behind on a glowing little *brasero* of charcoal, we sup. Boatmen and passengers are in a hurry to go. We must reach Ajutchitlán — which is another good six hours down the river — this same night. Meanwhile, here is beer, that great blessing of Tierra Caliente — good beer from Orizaba; a deep plate of frijoles, steaming, with fresh cheese, and tortillas which have just been toasted; then a whole half chicken, broiled. Afterwards, good black coffee, grown in this village, as is the brown sugar served with it. We pay — it amounts to about twelve cents (American) for each of us — and we are off for the boat. The boatmen are all drunk, but it makes little difference. There is a marvellous moon tonight. We move miraculously downstream, passing under great cliffs like sphinxes in silver, and the big fellow from the coast tells a story of five years in jail somewhere in Chihuahua and the boatmen sing bawdy songs. The rest of us smoke, or sit, listening.

" *Ari la cucha* " says the Doña Antonina in a mixture of Tarascan and bad Spanish, as Serafín — we later call him the *guachi* (equivalent in this idiom to " brat ") — chases a pig across us where we lie on petates under the *zapote* tree in her yard. The house is just there. It has walls of woven twigs, neatly plastered with mud. Its high, saddle-shaped roof of palm thatch extends shade all the way to where we are and embraces beneath it a kitchen with a most elegant stove for charcoal of smooth dried mud — handsome — and a sort of gallery with a hammock slung between strangely twisted columns, which are gnarled trunks of trees. The floor is of mud, also smooth, packed by the passage of bare feet. And the whole establishment, including the patio, is enclosed by a barricade of thorn and cane. A burro is tied just back of us. There are two strangely

naked black dogs — must be *tecezquintles,* the ancient Aztec type. They have no hair on their feet, bodies, their tails, or their ears. Only a few stray strands, which give a funny expression, over the eyes. There is a duck in a mud hole three feet away from us and above, in the *bugambilia* two little green *periquitos* are pluming and billing each other. Just beyond the barricade, visible through the slits in the

AJUTCHITLÁN

fence, is the pebbled bank and brown flood of the Río Balsas. Somewhere from beyond the other side of the patio bells are being rung for mass in the church, which we have not yet seen. This, then, is Sunday, and we are in Ajutchitlán.

Ajutchitlán is large. The church is a crumbling old pile from the sixteenth century. There is also a chapel, with cherubs like an Indian conception of a

circus; there are two spacious plazas with plenty of shade, surrounded by beautiful white arcades with vistas into patios now overgrown with weeds. The big houses are all vacant. . . . The Revolution passed this way. . . . There are bars across *zaguán* gates and tall grilled windows are heavily shuttered. They are being slowly forgotten, along with the pre-revolution families who once lived in them, now scattered and broken. And the big dusty streets

are mostly empty. The rest of Ajutchitlán spreads
out over the hills in the direction of the Sierra de la
Tentación. The houses are all like that of the Doña
Antonina, of grass and palm and twigs and mud.
The people here live simply. They have remained
close to the soil. They wash themselves in the river
and plant their little patches of corn and frijol each
family for itself. And in the dry season they make
pottery, using water and mud from the banks of the
Balsas, and they sell it in villages but slightly farther
removed.

In the next patio people are painting unbaked
clay. *Cántaros* and *cazuelas,* elegantly fashioned, for
water, and *zahumerios* for burning incense of copal,
done in deep tones of green — some brilliant with a
fine hard glaze — stand in rows on the smooth earth
floor of the yard. They say they are getting ready to
set out for Pungarabato. The market will be Thurs-
day. They will pack all these things on burros and
on their own backs as well. In a Fifth Avenue window one of these tall *incensarios* would cause a sensation; except that these people are unconscious that
that Fifth Avenue Art exists. Their most ambitious
pieces will probably sell in Pungarabato for about
eight cents. They will return on foot to Ajutchitlán
feeling themselves well paid.

The Doña Antonina has some more things —
which she calls common stuff — to show us, which

are made in Changato. That is the next village to-ward Coyuca de Catalán. The stuff is so fine, so pure in drawing, and so intensely Mexican in spirit that it can only be compared in character with the pre-colonial codices that hang in the National Museum. But this is modern. And innocent of imitation of antiques. . . . We must bring some of these things back with us.

We are off on burros for two or three days back up the river and by the opposite bank. The guachi be-comes our *arriero*, our mule-driver, and he has prob-ably never been so pleased about a job before, not in all his fifteen years. He sings and digs his heels into the burro's belly, throws stones at birds and, prac-tising with his rope, worries his poor beast all day long, lassoing him by one leg, then another. At in-tervals he relates long accounts of mountains and caves and ghosts and dances. We pause in San Miguel and have a warm bottle of beer, then set out again for barren hills and El Cubo, somewhere across the Balsas. They say there is an ancient tem-

ple there, and an old man who has idols he wants
to sell. We lose our way, sleep on the river bank,
are picked up by some boatmen who collect fifteen
centavos for ferrying us, burros and all, to the opposite shore. El Cubo is lost in a maze of underbrush and mesquite. There are no paths, but we
finally arrive. One night in a cantina, and the next
morning the old man with the idols. He is a charm-
ing old fellow, and he happens to think that his few
crude sculptures and little *idolos* are worth any price
he may name. Therefore he asks five thousand pesos.
(Any sum beyond the price of a sarape or a horse
is all the same to these people.) Then he asks two
hundred pesos. But he finally turns down my offer of
ten pesos cash, and we depart with effusive leave-
takings and a slight feeling of futility on both sides.
Next week the old devil will probably sell the things
to the keeper of the cantina for two pesos.

The temple, not far away, is a large and slightly
vague mass. It is perhaps three hundred by one hundred and fifty feet and is at least fifty feet to the
upper terrace. It crowns a low hill by the river where
the cactus and mesquite have reduced it to an inde-
terminate ruin. Here is work for archaeologists. We
leave it to press onward, planning to cross the river
at Comelagarto and return by another route.

Ten hours later, after crossing table lands and
rock-strewn hills, the beer is good in San Miguel
Totolapan. . . . So good, that from there to Ajut-

chitlán the four hours pass with a comfortable sense of timelessness, hills smoothed out, and a sort of enduring good humour . . . God's gift to Tierra Caliente! The guachi is sleeping in the saddle.

The guachi wants to go to Pungarabato with us. His mother weeps and says if the boy goes he will never come back, and what will she do without his support . . . will we give her a peso — a single *fierro*. We go to the *capilla,* the chapel, to look at the *teponaxtle* (a pre-Conquest drum of carved wood) which they still use in their religious dances.

Shouts from the river. A boat on its way to Pungarabato. Vamos! — Vamos! We run to make it, gathering sarapes and paints and pistols from the jacal as we go. The guachi joins us with a whoop. Having been bathing himself in the river, he doesn't pull on his ragged calzones until we are in the boat, from which he screams "adios" — and some other details in Tarascan — to his mother, while he stands shining and naked on the bow.

Adios to Ajutchitlán. Doña Antonina rushes down to the pango, bringing us a green censer as a gift. She expects us back next year. Her bare feet are in the water as she waves adios with her brown hands.

The mayordomo, who looks like a kind bandit in the form of a buzzard, is tight. It is his saint's day.

Little by little the others get under way. Between them they have two bottles. One is mezcal, mixed with green chili. The other, strangely, is a bottle of port wine, *legítimo*. For them it is all the same, but when my turn comes I choose the port. At Tlapehuala we all have a couple of rounds of the superb XX beer. The sacks of sugar, boxes of Cigarros Número Doce, and several rolls of barbed wire are tottered ashore here through mud to above the knees. Then we are off. . . . Follow the rapids.

The stream divides here to join again a half mile below. To the right goes the body of the river toward great rocks and a series of churning falls. To the left branches a sort of long steep mill-race, where there are rocks, but concealed, producing only a sort of magnified corduroy on the swift surface of the stream. This course we take. The pango enters the mill-race, and the mayordomo drinks to his craft. He shouts deliriously, *" Déjalo! . . . a poco no se va bien solito. . . ."* (" Let's see where she lands unaided! ") The boat, like an awkward girl at her first dance, goes sideways, then tail first. The current catches her on her side and we are rushed downstream at a dizzy speed. There is one, then another, then a dozen terrific blows on the bottom of the coffin-like craft. The performance lasts a good ten minutes, then we arrive, spewed into calm waters, miraculously intact. The mayordomo, in a mezcal-

choked voice, starts singing *Allá en el rancho grande*, but soon collapses in a drooling mass in the place where the cargo has been.

We are about to arrive in Pungarabato. From here there will be six long days mule-back to Toluca in the state of Mexico. And about the same through Michoacan to the railroad at Valladolid or Uruapan. We are on the northwestern limits of Guerrero. Only the river of Cutzamala separates us now from Michoacán. And to get back to Taxco there are five or six days of from ten to fourteen hours a day in the saddle over the highest sierras of the state of

Guerrero. . . . We will rest here a few days, then go back by Tanganhuato and Tlapehuala to Arcelia. From there by Almoloya and Arroyo Seco, stopping at Acapetlahuaya, then Buena Vista, Teloloapan and Los Sabinos and out by the Canyon de los Sabinos to Ahuehuepan and Iguala. From there Taxco lies due north on the highway from Acapulco to the Capital.

We feel ourselves incredibly remote from the world.

We are a full hour on foot in the dusk reaching Pungarabato from the river. And another half hour tramping long streets where closely built huts of jacal, straw thatching, follow each other interminably, before reaching our inn and the plaza. The air is still hot after what has been a long blazing day on the river. *Oye joven,* listen boy, where to find a bottle of beer? . . . Just there, across the plaza, señor — where the electric light is! Arriving at the indicated point we find a *nevería*. It is a shop with electric light plant, an engine puffing away somewhere in the patio — an ice-plant — and beer of the best waiting for us on ice.

The proprietor, an Arab, offers me a Mexico City newspaper which has just arrived. It is nine days old. And then he says if I am an American perhaps I would like to hear San Antonio. What is San Antonio? The jazz they make in San Antonio, Texas, señor. Then he goes in and starts a radio. What a town, this Pungarabato!

It is very dark. I am on a big galloping grey mule and the *mozo* is on another. We are off three hours before daylight, bound due west, destination Huetamo. He says it will take six hours only, but they develop into ten. Three hours of hard riding, mostly in the black before daylight; then we pause to breakfast at Los Cueramos. Later there are razor-backed hills of brutal grey rock laid on edge. Just ahead is the Pass — it is called Malpaso — famous for hold-ups. Travellers, says the mozo, are held up here regularly, according to custom. The agrarians in these parts are bad. There has been no rain, and consequently no crops for the past two years. Corn, if not raised, must be bought.

But nothing happens. The mozo rides with *carabina* across saddle, like the agraristas. The Pass is narrow and fantastic, a mere split in the saddle of one of those big grey mountains. Vast cliffs rise sheer from the trail and the path is obscured with dense vegetation. There are orchids of various hues, like jaws of voracious animals in miniature, and much organ cactus. Almost everything has spines, except the big white-blooming *cueramo* trees. On the other side it all turns suddenly arid again, the scene quivering into hot distances.

Huetamo is bigger than Ajutchitlán or Pungarabato, and more beautiful and more desolate. This was once the kingdom of the Tarascans. Pyramids and ruined temples at Cútzeo, and Cuirícuaro near by, bear witness, as do certain designs, that the Indians there still carve for themselves on gourds of *tecomate*. But nowadays most of them are agraristas and more preoccupied with robbing each other of lands than with decorating gourds.

Washing the dust from my face in the pool in the patio of the little inn in Huetamo, someone greets me from his hammock on the other side. *"Hola chico! Qué andas haciendo por acá?"* ("Hello, young fellow! What are you doing around here?") It is the old fellow from the boat, that first day down the Balsas — he of the opera glasses and the green umbrella — *el pobre doctor*.

We embrace each other and then enthusiastically sit down to compare notes. The poor old doctor has arrived at Huetamo by chartering another pango below Coyuca and then coming up by mule from Zirizicuaro. He was seventeen hours from Zirizicuaro here and the arrieros held him up for twenty-five pesos. *"Y que le parethe esho, chico?"* — for he is Spanish — ("How does that seem to you?")

Next day, a late start. Nine hours riding, and we arrive back at Pungarabato. The nevería, Arab in attendance, is still there to welcome us. . . . And that marvellous cold beer!

Three days from Pungarabato and we are climbing, climbing, climbing. Formidable ranges. Pity the poor horses. Still it is better for them than the steep down-going. We have bought lacquered *jícaras,* flat gourd bowls for basins, in Tlapehuala, got tight in Arcelia and slept two more nights on the floors of various huts. At Arroyo Seco there were torrential rains. Passing in the dark one of the horses was nearly lost in the stream. At Almoloya, for five pesos we bought from an innkeeper a stone mask, like the one in the National Museum that is incrusted with turquoise. . . . And all those villages there, unsuspected, hidden in the vast folds of the Sierra Madre — along the backbone of the continent. . . . In Acapetlahuaya we found a new type of lacquer, as fine and distinguished in design and technique as the now famous lacquer of Olinalá, but entirely distinct. The hybiscus, birds, vines, and fabulous tigers, painted with a fine gum lacquer, amazingly stylized. . . . Above Acapetlahuaya toward Buena Vista, we stumbled on the ruins of a once well fortified city of the ancients. Streets and passageways, cut out of the solid rock, foundations of many buildings, all of laboriously cut stone, constructed sometime long before the conquest. . . . We passed on to Buena Vista. From here the view actually dominates all Tierra Caliente. Only at this height it is quite cool again. Below are the vast creases of the valleys of the Cordillera. They fall away from us toward the plains of Ajutchitlán and Pungarabato. Over there rises the same Cerro del Aguila, now a mere jagged spur in the direction of the home of our friend the guachi. *" Allí está! allí está mi tierra! "* he points, grinning. In the blue haze are the barely visible coils of that monster Río Balsas. It shines, faintly opalescent. And beyond rises the pointed profile of the Sierra de la Tentación and the Unexplored Region. . . . Adiós, Tierra Caliente! The guachi twists the hair of his burro, neatly, just under the saddle on his rump. The animals plod on over the divide toward Teloloapan and Iguala. Another two or three days of this and we will be back in Taxco. We turn in our saddles to follow the flight of an eagle in the barranca below and for a last look at the magnificent perspective of Tierra Caliente.

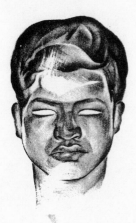

In the early morning, while Popocatepetl is still a blue paper cutout against the light of a not-yet-visible sun, we are off for a village a few hours farther north. Don Leopoldo believes that since we are neither federal agents nor Zapatistas, the old patriarchs there will consent to show us their ancient documents. . . . Rumour has it that there is a mapa antiguo, *more than two metres square, painted on hand-woven cloth. It must be one of those pictorial Aztec documents which record incidents contemporary with the conquest — graphic chronicles made for the eyes of the king in Tenochtitlan (yet to be called the City of Mexico) — for Moctezuma or Cuauhtemoc. The final ascent to this well-guarded place is a matter of a two hours' steady climb — exhausting. We arrive in the middle of the day and push through a small group of lounging soldiers to*

enter the cantina and drink warm beer. Beyond the brief plaza the land drops away, as from the edge of a table, and there are only the brutal shapes of iron-grey mountain ranges in outline. A little conversation and Don Leopoldo and his compadre *go off to fetch the documents. . . . A young soldier, drinking mezcal, bursts forth with a few gratuitous curses and* groserías — *just for the general effect. . . . They bring a small manuscript, written in Aztec, which appears to be — according to Don Trinidad — an account of Hernan Cortes' arrival at this place. There is a large manuscript, each page stamped with* Felipe Quinto, REY DE ESPAÑA, *dating roughly from the early part of the eighteenth century. It concerns the struggles of our friend Don José de la Borda for the mineral rights to some several hundreds of square miles of territory — the same silver grandee who built Taxco and who owned the richest mines in Mexico. There being almost no available data on his life, the document is particularly fascinating. . . . But the third piece is by far the most interesting — the " picture-map." Don Trinidad has it folded into a homemade sheepskin binding with raw-hide clasps. It is on old cotton cloth the colour of pale tea. . . . Lively battles, large groups of seated figures, quite evidently portraits of principal citizens, and pictured rivers-like-snakes, green mountains like woven beehives, the placing of some forty ancient cities (many now non-existent). One of them*

*is Tetipac, where we plot thirteen stone edifices —
all that and more went into the painting of this brave
codex. . . . To be exact, this is the more than four
hundred year old title of these people to a vast territory.*

*Half the town comes to watch as I set to work on a
big table under the portales to make a copy of this
thing. . . . The boy who has been drinking in the
shop comes out to see, too. "Hola!—— tu madre!" he brings out, arm over my shoulder. But I am
too busy to keep up the conversation, though I remember he has become very sentimental about
Guanajuato, where he was conscripted for the army.
. . . The schoolmaster comes to invite me for a cup
of black coffee. There are three other soldiers, rifles
lowered in hand, approaching the first. "We are taking you to jail," they are telling him. "Why? . . .
No, por mis ——" "I am not going!"-. . . And
now, just as I put my cup down and turn back, one
of the soldiers raises his rifle and shoots him, at less
than a yard away. He falls, almost at my feet, groans
once, then rolls over on his face. There is a big
spot of bright blood spreading on the white of his
shirt between the shoulder blades, exactly in the centre of his back. . . . There is a small sapling, evidently recently planted by the school-children, just
back of where the boy had stood. One of the soldiers, noticing a notch in it made by the shot, remarks with a smile, "Un recuerdito,"—"A little*

souvenir of the day!" . . . The old men are silent, ashamed of the thing. Only old Trinidad remarks to me aside, with a shrug of his shoulders, ". . . the army, señor!"

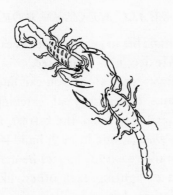

TIERRA FRIA

YSAÍAS — Isaiah, in biblical terms — amuses himself catching *alacranes*. It is while we are waiting for more rope to reach the cave. This country is pure limestone — limestone turned on end and dressed with a few scrawny palmettos. The hill has been pushed upward, like a dome. It is as full of holes as a Swiss cheese. Many of them are good-sized caves, though most difficult to find. Ysaías knows all about them, shows us entrances that look like swallows' nests, that go downward smoothly, like a funnel, without a handcatch, and then open suddenly out into vaulted chapels, with chasms and more chapels far below. It is very exciting. We have already come across a few potsherds and are hoping for something more complete. Floyd Collins would have had the time of his life here. Particularly if he had had the archaeological urge. Or perhaps his urge was just caves. . . . Anyway, this is Mexico, not Tennesseé.

Under almost every stone you can find the wicked animals. Ysaías has a way of catching them just back of the head. He takes the fattest, most glistening ones, the *gueros*, one in each hand — if their little fish-hook tails reach his fingers he may die — and he puts them to fighting each other, like two game cocks in miniature. Little by little, the scorpions become more warlike. When he finally puts them down on the top of a limestone slab, they fall to fighting in deadly earnest. This is better than a cockfight. With tiny lobster-like pincers they clinch and loosen grips. The tails, loaded with their creamy poison, whip in and out, seeking the opportunity to inject death. At last it happens. The one injected fights clear and departs haltingly, the other disdaining to follow — knowing well his adversary cannot survive for more than a minute. Ysaías is delighted. He pulls the sting off the live one and offers to eat him. No one insists, but he eats him anyhow. What I wish is that we had made a movie close-up of the battle.

We enter the cave. I go first, the rope around my waist, because the hole is too smooth to get even a toe-hold. At the bottom, sixty feet below, is a mud floor. A narrow tunnel leads off one end which we must go through on our bellies. There is another drop, very difficult, about forty feet. I land on one side of an enormous cavern. There are no more passageways. If there have been any, they were long ago filled up with the accumulated earth. Here we find charred wood, a handful of *tepalcates* — potsherds — and a distinguished jar, fairly large, which has in it a few jadeite beads and two little bronze hatchets. Here is what we were looking for. The jar not only furnishes a sort of prototype for the pottery

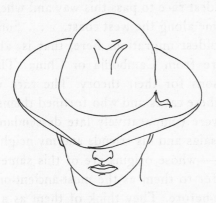

they make nowadays in Huapam below here, but it has a beautiful design with stepped angles and is unmistakably late Aztec, proving that trade existed between these parts and the Aztec capital in Mexico; that this was not a race of barbarians; and that they enjoyed the cultural stimulus of Moctezuma's artisans.

Heretofore this part of Mexico — this western half of the country — has been referred to only as " Nahua." No one has distinguished the different civilizations that existed here before the conquest, nor outlined the extent of influence of the known pre-Hispanic cultures; that is to say, just how far southward and westward the Aztecs dominated, or how far north the Zapotecs reached, or far eastward along the Balsas river the Tarascan civilization penetrated. And, back of it all is the question of what was the oldest race to pass this way and whether the Mayas came along the west coast. . . . Some think that the oldest migrations here, that is, along the coast, were from Cambodia or China. There are good reasons for their theory. The race who hid things in these caves and who fortified themselves in Tetipac were comparatively late descendants, even though Ysaías and his friends and my neighbours in the town — whose origins are of this same race — like to refer to them as the most-ancient-ones-who-have-gone-before. They think of them as a race of giant builders-in-stone, who lived so long ago that they had nothing to do with what is now Mexico. Whereas, you have only to look at the faces of Tata Luis, of Doña María de la Luz, of Ysaías, in order to realize their background.

The light is failing. The remains of storm clouds leave great ragged patches of indigo with only brief patches of faded blue between. We are on the steepest part of the ascent, the part where, looking back over the horse's rump, you begin to feel suspended between the above and the below. Directly beneath us are the stony reaches of the cave country just explored. The domes and towers of Tetipac are becoming blurred, but the fields of corn and cane, even at this distance, retain shades of moist green in rectangular patterns. Back of us, to the south are piled the mountains of Guerrero, with the Huitzteco dominant and massive on the horizon. It is strange to realize that the town is just beyond that big peak and that in this short while we have actually, tortuously circumnavigated those heights.

The sarape is wet across my shoulder. As I throw it off to roll it, the horse starts — it is at a point precipitously dangerous. Ysaías, just ahead of me, throws back his head and laughs. The old man on the white mule ahead, the ancient Don Carmen, very deaf, looks back complacently and says with a wave of his hand toward the rocks above, *Sí, Sí*. We're arriving, we're arriving! Then he smiles sadly and innocently and we resume attention to the laboured movements of our beasts and the uncanny instinct which guides them. Being near the end of the search and just a little sceptical, having no idea what marvels may lie on the mesa just above, I am not too tired to be vaguely excited. On other trips I have already scrutinized the outlines of this mountain of Tetipac from a distance. Twice I have been told by Indians that there was a great city, the ruined city of the most-ancient-ones-who-have-gone-before, up there on its summit. The Department of Archaeology in the capital told me there had been nothing noted on their maps about this place. But even if three hundred new archaeological sites a year are discovered in Mexico, this country will remain but slightly known, for a long time to come. The Indians are always a little fantastic when they talk about

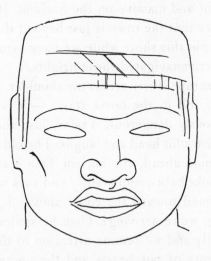

these things. They tell you what they think you would like to hear. One of them told me that here in Tetipac-el-Viejo, as they call this mountain top, there was an emerald, a clear green emerald, of which only he knew the whereabouts. With his hands he indicated a stone the size of a packing box. What he was probably thinking of was obsidian. But since he was drunk, what difference!

Our path becomes almost a chimney, winding
steeply up between perpendicular towers of rock.
There are only two points of accessibility to the mesa
and this is the most direct. Emerging at the top is
like coming through onto a vastly elevated floor. It
is cold. The white mule ahead, with the old man in
his ragged blanket, plods on unhurried over fields

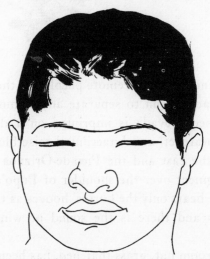

of brown straw which alternate with areas of flat
rock, barren except for lichens. Above us the rock
rises to higher levels.

As we round a jut of rock the volcanoes show
themselves. All four are in plain view, distant and
detached, as though painted. The valley of Toluca
stretches fully seventy miles to the north, a pale
blue haze out of which the distant lights of Malinal-

tenango and the more remote pueblos of the Otomis have already begun to separate and shimmer. The snow-capped Nevada is imprinted on a darkening sky. Popocatepetl and Ixtaccihuatl raise blue shapes away to the east and the Pico-de-Orizaba is but a faint fragment over the shoulder of Popo's perfect cone. One hears only the horses' hooves as they clink on stones and there is the sound of wind in .the grass.

A one-room hut, grass-thatched, has been built on the floor formed by an inverted dome of clean rock. In this country of jacales, of woven twigs and palm thatch, more rarely of adobe, there is one thing re-markable about this house: it is extraordinarily well built of carefully laid cut stone, without mortar.

While Ysaías takes care of the horses I try to talk to the old man. We squat on a log and wait for the kitchen to arrive. Don Carmen has told me that his

DON CARMEN

daughters had thought it would be best simply to move the kitchen, since we are to be here two, three, or even four days. After a while, they come, two great, quiet-featured women. In the village they had spoken of them — almost with awe — as the " big women of Don Carmen." The kitchen itself is no more than a stone metate, a few earthenware pots, corn, frijoles, etc. It is all packed on the back of a burro.

But conversation fails to flourish. The old man is amiable — and completely absent-minded. He is plainly beyond the stage of taking a lively interest in anything. Idols, to him, are just funny things you pick up in the fields, of no importance except to children and foreigners. (A man from Mexico City would be as much a foreigner here as one from London.) Some people he knows are superstitious about these things. He has a cousin who has a death's-head in blue stone, and that cousin puts the death's-head to guard his corn. Not only that, but every year he kills his biggest turkey and puts its blood in a bowl before the idol. (That must have been the god Teocuitle.) But he prefers telling me of how he got possession of this mesa during the revolution. He can raise a little corn on it and occasionally, over on the forested peak of La Estrella, or the Cerrohuates, he can shoot a deer. And sometimes wild boar come this way.

According to civilized schedules it is not yet late

when Ysaías and I gather petates and sarapes and go off to sleep in a little shack we have spotted on the next rise. It has a layer of canes laid on the rafters and we, or rather I, have decided it will be a good place for the night. Ysaías keeps saying something about uninhabited houses and the little animals. But the cane platform is inviting and with the petate it should be almost soft. There is a slender tree trunk, notched, leaned in the corner as a ladder.

As we crawl up over the edge, the boy with his miner's lamp in advance, I feel his position suddenly stiffen. Chinning myself to the edge I make out a glistening coil of black-and-white-and-vermilion.

The eyes of the snake glisten, too, as he sways his head toward us and the light. Having only our machetes, we back out hot foot. Returning with stones, the *coralillo* is just disappearing into a crack in the wall at the eaves. And when we rush to meet him outside his coils are just twisting through the grass of the roof. The rocks drive him in and we finally kill him — it is working in cramped quarters — with a pole and more stones. Then we throw him outside the shack and sit down on the platform and laugh.

But the boy has one theme, which he reverts to: that when people quit a house the little animals come in. And grass roofs are supposed to be specially inviting. As he speaks, I glance up to scan the neatly woven roof above our heads. There are several small spiders and one like black velvet, as big as your hand — a tarantula, about two feet away. That settles it. We sleep in the open in the middle of a great flat rock. It is cold and there is only one petate, a straw mat, between us and the rock. Our two sarapes are combined against the brittle night air. It is better out here. We sleep. The smooth warmth of my friend's body through his thin cotton is near and pleasant. About us now, in place of coralillos and tarantulas, there are only a moon and stars. Also the remote forms of unknown mountains.

Tetipac-el-Viejo, this impregnable mountain top, many centuries ago must have been the citadel of a hard warlike race. There are several ruins, some of considerable size, all of cut stone. On the central peak, La Juaca, are seven pyramidal structures and the remains of a broad masonry platform. Once they were plastered and painted a smooth red. On one of these platforms, now in the middle of a small milpa of Don Carmen's corn, are two beautifully carved gods. They probably had to do with creation and fertility. The male figure, in the best Aztec tradition, has an ear of corn in his left hand and some sort of insignia in his right.

In the fields of the mesa just below are thousands of bits of tepalcates, obsidian knives, arrow heads, domestic utensils, broken metates and metlapiles, identically like those made in Piedras Negras today, and pieces of painted pottery which show that trade relations existed with the valley of Toluca. We fill our sacks of ixtle fibre with potsherds. Of more elegant objects there is scarcely anything. A few broken figurines in clay. Ysaías calls it a *mina de muñecas* — a doll mine.

The ruins themselves are so utterly demolished, particularly the important ones, that it is only with great difficulty that I can make out enough for pencilled notes of plans. So complete a destruction puzzles me.

The ancient Don Carmen takes little interest in what we do. It is hard to talk with him because one has to shout. He sits in the sun and squints and mutters things. Or smiles sympathetically when he sees us smiling. Though he is even innocent of the strange noises he himself makes at times, he always smiles and nods when he sees Ysaías grin.

But *hombre,* I say to him along toward the evening of the third day, you promised me that we would come across all sorts of decorations, stone masks, of the most-ancient-ones-who-have-gone-before, and there is hardly a single one to be seen!

He seems to be slowly, painfully remembering something. Ah, sí! he says vaguely, getting up and beginning to survey the wall at his back. Perhaps his mind is wandering a little. He is pointing with a shaking hand to the wall. There, there he is! — do you see him? Built into the unplastered wall is the crude head of a Nahua idol. Then in another part is a section of a gigantic plumed serpent. And then we go inside and discover in its obscurity a few more stone carvings, mostly heads, built into the walls as casually as blocks of adobe, except that some of the heads are upside down. The rest of the walls are of cut stone, with clean square corners.

The old man, a little uncertain of my interest, is explaining that all this rock was carried here by hand. He says it came from the ruins they call the " *igle-sia*." That was the temple of this old city we have been digging in. . . . The facts of Tetipac-the-ancient, then, are present in these walls, but inarticulately. The sensation is as though someone, with a few careless strokes, had deliberately erased from before your eyes all traces of the city of the most-ancient-ones-who-have-gone-before.

Even here in the fiesta they are incredibly quiet. But there is an undercurrent of real gaiety about the scene. People are smiling, are drinking their atole *or* pulque *or eating their* taquitos *or fruit. If it is evening there will be singers on the street and in the cantinas, wandering troubadours with a guitar and perhaps a companion with violin or bass viol. . . . They sing the* corridos, *those long and moving ballads which the people love. One stops to listen, fascinated. . . . Later in the evening there will be the inevitable fireworks — rockets and, above all, the bulls.*

These formidable little bulls, made of rawhide, painted and highly charged with hand-made explosives, mounted on the heads of men, will dance into the crowds, will charge from the church steps into the plaza and strike terror and ecstasy into the hearts of all. Some will have their calzones catch fire, women will be terrified — but all will be overflowing with good humour. . . . Perhaps there will be a castillo, *a firework castle, which is a deafening and magnificent affair. Then children will scream with delight and men and women will give way before the shower of golden and coloured fire.* Espléndido! — Ay, qué bonito! — Estupendo! *It is an overwhelming event. Words fail. After that all go home. . . . All, that is, except the Indian lads who have already wrapped themselves in their sarapes and laid themselves to sleep there on the cobbles on the far side of the plaza. And there will linger a few reeling bo-rrachos, desperately grasping their bottle of* tequila *or* mezcal, *and some others over by the cantina singing, perhaps planning a* gallo — *they will serenade until early morning. And then, in the* mañanita — *before actual dawn — the drums will already be throbbing and these men and their brothers will be sombrely moving in the rhythmic swing and turn and clash of* machetotes *of the dances. . . . The spirit of the Fiesta Mexicana fills and sustains them.*

FIESTA MEXICANA

TO witness a fiesta for the first time — a real one, where the people have come from all the little villages of the mountains above and from the hot distant plains of Tierra Caliente below — is to see Mexico. To rub shoulders with the Indian population, to see them smiling and occupied, eating their simple meals, arguing agrarian problems over a cup of tequila, arranging themselves on the ground for the night, and, above all, to witness their dances and to observe the mystery of the faces of the dancers — is a profound experience and one not easily described afterwards. These things have to do with the race itself. One must realize that the fiesta derives from its own mysterious impulse and continues year after year, having survived the conquest; that announcement of it in metropolitan dailies is unnecessary; that it remains perfectly known, like an ancient formula, to all good Mexicans of the provinces.

At Tepalcingo last year there were eleven groups of dancers, intent, monotonous in their rhythms, dancing in the heavy dust or in the quiet shade of the vast atrium of the church. It was a sixteenth century church with Aztec Sun and Moon, each about ten feet in diameter, cut in the pink stone wall of the two great towers. . . . I thought it the most Mexican church I had ever seen. . . . The dancers were both inside the building and out.

The kings of the Moors and Christians are nearest to where we are. Their dance lasts three days and acts out some ancient story. It is a curious story, a little bit silly, very complicated and entirely beyond the realm of logic. But the dancers, intensely absorbed in the movement of their dance, are unconscious of theme or of the lengthy haranguing of chiefs who speak magic Aztec words.

Their grace is entirely masculine, strangely brutal in the lack of any hip movement. There is a simple rapidity of foot, swing, sharp turn and clash of swords (machetotes) above and below — whirl — clash — swinging — weaving, in and back; the dance goes on to a thin dry music of drums and flutes in three notes, and the dust rises and hovers as in an ancient battle.

KINGS OF THE MOORS AND CHRISTIANS

All this for the unique benefit of the local saint, which, like those of thousands of other villages, has great fame as a worker of miracles. Nuestro Señor, he of the saintly, bloody image, embroidered shirt, lace drawers, and crown of golden thorns, fallen there with his cross beside the altar, must indeed have been pleased.

More significant of the Indians who made them — more important to Mexico than plaster saints in marbleized niches — are the masks for these dances. Tiger masks, masks of old men, of the Moors, of the devil, of Death, and of Time. In some, the likeness to Xipe and other gods of the Ancient Aztecs and to those of their priests and their warriors is definitely there, if unconsciously achieved.

The masks are carved from solid trunks of the tree, Zompantle, which was for the Aztecs the Sacred-Tree-of-the-Dead. The paint with which the masks are decorated is prepared, more often than not, from pure earth colours, which are dug, when needed, in the mountains. Angel Ayala has shown me where he obtains his own reds and yellows — in marvellous tones — on the slopes of Huitzteco. Also in the country around here are many *zompantle* trees. In November, the month of the day of the dead, these trees are barren of leaves but are covered with brilliant, hard red beads, like drops of blood. . . . One wonders if the legend of this blood is not more

convincing to modern Aztecs than that of the painted blood of gilded Christs.

Times and seasons for the fiestas are inexplicably merged with the traditional celebration of the harvest; with the day of Tonanzintla, mother of the gods, or, it may be, with the period just before the rainy season. There is the Feast of the Day of the Dead (with us, All Souls' Day) and so on. The day of the patron saint of a village is, in each locality the excuse for the principal fiesta of the year, the degree of attraction depending on the saint's reputation for miraculousness. Thus thousands of remote, half-forgotten mountain villages become the scene of magnificent eight and fifteen day fiestas. And hundreds of thousands of Indians make accustomed pilgrimages to their favourite saints annually. . . . It would be more than futile to try to explain these things, these fiestas so full of conviction, so natural and impulsive, and so childlike, on the basis of sociological phenomena.

In Tecalpulco, an hour below here, the great fiesta is the first week in Lent. It is famous all the way from the Pacific coast to the plains of Puebla. In June comes the fiesta of the *Virgen de la Luz* (whose powers have to do with Tonantzintla and fertility). In Tixtla, in the more remotely mountainous section of Guerrero in the direction of Olinalá, there is a great fiesta and fair in September. This is for the Virgin of Los Remedios and lasts for fifteen eventful days. In March, there is a fiesta with roping of bulls, *jaripeo,* and all, in Acamixtla. Also in Huitztac. And toward the end of that month is the marvellous fifteen day fiesta of Our Lord of the Holy True Cross here in this town. The planting season and the rains inevitably follow closely on that event. . . . Farther away, toward the north, is Chalma, the most revered shrine in all Indian Mexico. There, in a small village hidden in the corrugations of the Sierra, are celebrated innumerable saints' days throughout the year. From time to time the streets of Taxco are thick with caravans of pilgrims, with their burros, children, and cooking utensils, en route to Chalma. It is a convincing sight.

About the dances themselves. Some are *antiquísimas,* handed down by word of mouth for generations on generations. Others are simply invented or are commenced as pantomimes in order to celebrate or properly chronicle a noteworthy local event. Thus, the dance of the Moors and Christians and the dance of the Tiger are very old, whereas the dance they principally celebrate in the little town of San Juan de las Naranjas near here is nothing more or less than the narration of the fall of a certain wicked bandit who had ravaged that region and was finally slain. Others are based on the function of the ancient oficios or trades. There are the dances of the arrieros, drivers of burro trains; of the Vaqueros, the cattle raisers; of the Tecomates, the weavers; of the

Tlacoleres, which is about those who carry food to the miners. In one, *chicotes,* cat-o'-nine-tails, are used and the dance is sometimes referred to as the dance of the Chicoteros. For this, sombreros are specially woven, triple-thick, of palm, and the masks — of zompantle — are three times life size and very solid, so that they may bear the rain of blows which are given about the head. The dance is not sadistic, as it might appear; rather, its form is based on life in the days of the Spaniards, when men were driven to work in the mines by gangs of savage overseers. The masks for the Chicoteros still·represent Indian versions of the exaggerated and insensate masters of colonial Mexico — types which today rule only behind the counters of small commercial establishments — since the grandees of the silver mines have long ago disappeared.

Of all the ancient dances of Mexico, aside from the exceedingly primitive and savage ones of the Tarahumaras in the north, the *danza del tigre* — of the tigers, sometimes called *tehuanes* — has more *chiste* — is more amusing — and probably is more interesting ideologically, than any other single dance. Also more difficult to explain. I am convinced that few, even of those who take part in it, have any really clear idea of its significance or even of the consecutive story which it relates. There is a strange mixture of known and unknown Mexico in it. That is to say that more than half the dialogue takes place in Aztec.

It is performed thus even in certain towns like this one where Aztec has ceased to be spoken generally. (Though the small boy who waters my garden calls to his friends in *Mexicano,* as it is called, and there are villages two hours away where no other language is understood.)

The names of the principal characters in the dance are typically Aztec, and the idea about which it is woven is primitive in the extreme. Briefly, the theme is the hunt. The tiger, a boy in a magnificent mask made of zompantle, painted or lacquered, with tusks of wild boar and bristling whiskers made of the black and white quill-like hair of the same animal, clothed in yellow stuff with painted black spots (or circles, if jaguar) is pursued throughout the dance, in which the pursuit itself becomes a series of dance evolutions.

Among the characters are several *Viejos,* who are the hunters, and with them one Salvadorchi, the leader of the hunt. They are dressed as *hacendados,* or farmers. There are also doctors, servants, deers, dogs, *zopilotes* (buzzards), the latter parts being taken by small boys. All have their appropriate masks of zompantle, or, sometimes, of leather or even tin. And I once saw one made of dried comb of wild honey. There is also the part of an old woman, taken by the tallest man, who wears side curls, long skirts, and carries a rag doll on a stick. She, of course, is by way of comic relief. The dance itself is very serious. The old lady's business is to be frightened by the tiger, who, leaping and bounding, chases and beats her with his tail.

The music is of a single reed flute and a small

drum, a singularly monotonous series of sounds, rising and falling shrilly, produced by the two hands of the same maestro. The sound effect gives a rapid pulse to the dance which is unforgettable.

Salvadorchi greets his band with " *Haxcani canca,*

viejo el huehuestique! " — a strange mixture of
Aztec and bad Spanish: with that the dance begins.

The speeches from here on are equally full of
Aztec phraseology — a curious succession of ex-
hortations, challenges, and enigmatically repeated
verse, which is difficult or even impossible in transla-
tion. When the Juan Titilchi or Viejo Changuasle is
wounded by the tiger, there is a ceremony which con-
sists of feeling, and measuring, and finally curing
him, at the end of which all say, ". . . *mayeso, ce
bolsa, ce ome, yei, nahui, maccuili, chicuahui . . .
ce mayeso otro real mas para que aliviarosque
ase animalito*" counting. Then the doctors chant in
chorus:

> " *Adios, caneni huihuenchi!*
> *Adios, caneni huihuenchi!*
> *Donde te mordió lo tigre*
> *Donde te mordió lo tigre*
> *Sonque ni nitecani . . .*"

The formula is repeated many times, as a sort of
finale to various dance evolutions. The whole takes
about two hours, which, as Angel remarks, is about
as much violence as the dancers can sustain. The
tiger gets shot and the horde of Zopilotes and dogs
fall upon the carcass.

The *danza del tigre* is one of the few religious
dances which attract more spectators than dancers.
It is very popular here in the cool country as well as

in Tierra Caliente. And I have seen it staged in Pungarabato, on the Costa Grande, at Tecpan on the Pacific, and as far south as the state of Oaxaca. As a matter of fact, the Zapotec village of Tehuantepec is named for the *tehuan* — the tiger —

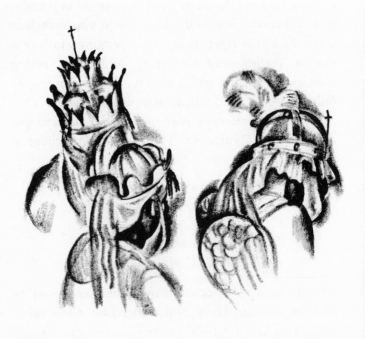

anciently an animal of very special significance in these parts.

But besides the dance of the tiger, which is always impressive, in spite of its monotony, there are many others equally popular, and worthy of note, such as the dances of the *Moros,* the *Tres Potencias* (Three Powers, also referred to as the Flesh and the Soul) and the special dance of the Little Roosters (which takes place once a year at the little church of Guada-

lupe on the hill above my house). . . . But they must be witnessed in order to appreciate what they mean when danced by these people. The colours for the legendary war between the Moors and the Christians are Indian colours, cerise and magenta and

pale and blue green. Perhaps there will be a priceless bit of sixteenth century brocade or cloth of gold
and silver borrowed from the sacristan sewed on a
garment somewhere. The kings will have flowing
brilliant capes and tall head-dresses, some like cres-
cents, others with plumes, and elegant, beautifully
wrought crowns of shining tin. And back of the
painted masks of Pilates and angels and warriors,
with carved beards and painted bloody slashes, can
be sensed the high dark cheekbones, the glint of un-
fathomable eyes of sturdy men from Tlamacuzapa
and Huiztac and Totolapan.

Approaching Tixtla on horseback we could hear
the clear measured voices of singing children rising
from the church. We were on top of one of those
enormous inverted-bowl-shaped mountains which
seem to get steeper as you approach the base. Tixtla
was hidden in the green of the plain far below.
There rose up toward us the clamour of bells
and there were the giant pops and blue puffs of
fireworks from the fiesta down there. Mingling
with these sounds as an undertone, the intermin-
able drums of the tiger dance made a sober background. But once we had arrived, everything seemed
comparatively quiet.

Most of the dances were being enacted among the
crowds in front of the church, and inside there were
at least three large groups. At first one could hardly

even see within the spacious red-tiled interior. The air was a blue haze, thick with the incense of copal, and the dim distances were punctuated by the faint glitter of hundreds of obscure candles clutched forward in the hands of the kneeling poor. Unques-

tioning Faith saturated the atmosphere — also the sweat of dancing warriors. There were the *pastorcitas,* little Indian girls with white veils and sombre faces, stolidly marching and retreating before the altar, carrying flower-festooned staffs and singing:

. . . *" vamos pastorcitas, vamos a Belén*
  Para ver al niño, a la Virgen también.
En Belén hay un bautismo, Bartolo vamos allá,
Si me quieren dar el bolo, que me lo traigan acá."

" Let us go, little shepherds, let us go to Bethlehem
  Let us go to see the Christ child, and also see the
    Virgin.
  In Bethlehem they are baptising, Bartolo do let's
    go,
  But if they wish to make me gifts, they must bring
    them to me now."

And now came the Moors and the Christians, solemnly dancing, and terminating at the steps of the
altar, making their adios to the Virgin, singing,
". . . *aora damos la salida vailando* " — now let us
make the departure dancing!

It was a sort of allegorical drama, with the dancers
in the role of unconscious actors, a drama in the
Greek sense in which the mere plot contains no
novelty for the audience.

II
PEOPLE

In the spring it is hot and dry. An opaque haze obscures barren mountain and brown plain. Though the fields have been laid open a month ago they lie fallow, awaiting the waters which are still six weeks off. There is still much corn in the family troje. Meanwhile, provident men cut new palmetto leaves or, if rich, acquire a few tiles for roofs that have rotted or may leak. It is a sign of the season to see *them perched on ridgepoles, children and all, white silhouettes against dark blue sky, weaving the covering that will protect for the year to come. New crosses of bamboos or carved wood will complete the new roofing and grant a benediction. And the idols which have lain all year in the corn troughs will be cleaned and put carefully back to guard the larder for another season. Those who have corn to spare will sell it for a good price at the spring fiesta in Tepalcingo or Tixtla or Tecalpulco.*

With the first rains comes feverish activity in the fields. They work from before daylight until after dark. New plows of massive oak have been made ready. The oxen, fat and sleek, and willing, are yoked and toil all day every day. Each family of the cuadrilla in turn is accorded use of the two great animals, owned communally. The land is opened for planting. Sometimes whole villages migrate to the fields, as in Texiuapan which is in the infertile folds of grey mountains. Kitchens and petates are carried down to the fields and rude shelters built in which they live until July or August, returning again in October or November for the harvest. It is a religious ritual, this annual embarkation, born in the race. Fruit of the soil comes to him who works it. Any other formula is unknown.

The summer is planting. After that comes rest. And, after that, the harvest. When the beasts come out of the fields and the labours are completed they make a quiet procession — except for the rockets — and a cup of mezcal is passed around. The oxen are decorated with little flags and looped chains of coloured paper as they come back to the homes that day. It is like finishing the structure of a house.

The harvest is the best. Corn and frijoles are sacked in ixtle and loaded to Iguala or the plaza in Taxco. Shares in the crop are paid off and there is plenty in the land. They buy a pig or a burro with the surplus. Or perhaps it is worth while to go to the horse fair at Totolapan or San Lucas. Thirty silver cartwheels will buy a decent horse there.

Then the long dry winter, with the heat becoming more intense. In that season one is dedicated to all the things one likes best to do; to the oficios of weaving new petates and the making of jars for guarding water. Gourds that have ripened and dried on roofs are taken down and lacquered with figures of little animals and the flower of the honeysuckle, in order to make a proper receptacle for the masa. Earth from the banks of the now drying rivers yields good adobe. Now, long before the waters come, young men with new families build houses. All this and much more happens during the dry season.

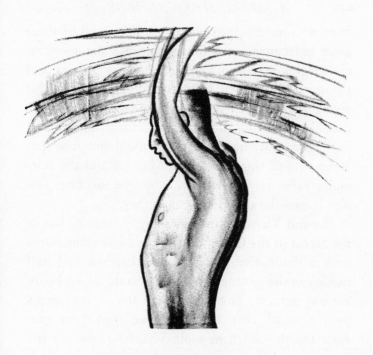

AGRARIAN

DON MÁXIMO BUSTAMENTE and the other colonial ones say it is silly for me to talk with the Indians. They say that it is probably all right for a foreigner, but that after all it is bad for my Spanish, which is still unpolished. They like to find fault with my use of the idiom and point out Indian terminations which I use from time to time. Not that it matters. And there are many among the Indians whose friendship has made life in Mexico very charming.

93

Men who have helped me on the house, all of them good craftsmen, carpenters, masons, and most of my neighbours, including the shoemaker Luis and the postmaster Don Eulalio. Among them is this young Juanito, who has done wonders with the garden. Naturally, on finding him and his wife, Victoria, in the plaza, we have things to talk about. And that is the sort of thing that Don Maximo and the coloniales refer to. Principally, I believe, because Juanito is considerably darker than they.

He and Victoria, and the baby, Atanasio, live in the Street of the Chachalacas. It is a one-room house with a diminutive gallery, palm-thatched and half hidden in the greenery of the barranca down below the old convent. The house is not theirs; they pay a peso a month rent, but they have lived there ever since the day when he stole Victoria from her employers, and they are very happy. Principally he is happy because there is a little strip of ground about the house where he can raise a few hills of corn and keep a pig and a few chickens. He is completely in love with the soil. He says there has never been a year since he was fourteen years old that he has not cultivated a field of corn somewhere in the hills beyond the town. He says there have been some good years and some bad, and he has never actually possessed a plot of ground, but that at least he with his own hands has always laid by enough corn to provide his family with tortillas through the dry season.

He is simple and warm-hearted and he has a feeling about plants and flowers. When you see him in the plaza on Sundays he invariably has a sprig of tuberose or jasmine behind his ear. And when he comes to visit he usually brings a bouquet, which he presents gravely, or some orchideous flowering plant or vine that he has discovered in the mountain, or else two or three ears of new corn. He has never dreamed of politics, or of speaking to the Doña Petra without raising his hat, and for him the revolution was a natural phenomenon, like one of these local earthquakes, which crack the walls of your house, but about which you can do nothing. He giggles if you make him speak Aztec, but there is nothing which so thoroughly delights his soul as to " come out " in one of the religious dances. More than anything else, he loves the Dance of the Tiger. He has been living here in the town the last few years, but that is only because a rich *diputado* who lives in Toluca stole the title to his father's share in the communal lands above here. Also, he makes good adobe and can sell it here.

He loves to stop by and talk. It happens that we are compadres, his Atanasio being my first god-child. We always talk about the *niño* and I listen to the things the child has almost said and how they purged him that morning, and then, with a little encouragement, he will go on to tell me the story of his life. He tells it like the narrations of an Aztec codex.

There is nothing particularly heroic about it and he becomes strangely involved in place-facts and events, interspersed with encounters with wild animals and witch-doctors. His dark face takes on an air of childlike absorption. He sits there on the gallery, or squats with his back against the fountain, and his voice as he talks is quite simple, almost monotonous.

BI'TORIA

These are the things the colonial ones think I am a fool to listen to:

. . . And I saw Bi'toria that day and I said, If you want to come with me and my mamá, that you come right now, today, and she said that yes and she came. She only brought her rags and they were beneath her rebozo. And now there are three years since that day and the boy-child is big and he talks. And that he pulls the pig by the ear! And that he laughs all the day, all the day! And in the year that enters he will go with me one day to see the *maíz* in my field below Pichagua. . . . I at the age of eight cared for the cattle in the mountain. They were oxen, colour of *súchil* and some black. I remember me very well. There was one called the Primavera and one was the Mariposa and they came, like dogs, when you called them. They belonged to Don Efrén Cuellar, a man well energetic. Yes, he was a little Indian. He had sugar cane which required fourteen teams of oxen to work it and he was well rich. He had twenty-four beef and two cows. In those days I was paid fifty centavos the week and my food, but it was very difficult to live on only one tortilla with salt a day. Don Efrén he said that frijoles were not necessary for a brat my size. But I had a small jar and sometimes I drove away the calf and I milked the cow and that I drink it! I was well small, thin, thin. My feet still carry scars from those days, because I had no *huaraches*. That was later. And the spines of the cactus spined me much. Then a big boar came at me one day, it was up there among the mezquite and the *tepehual* trees, and that I jump, but still he stepped my foot and my ankle and foot were much swollen. And another time the cows wandered into the vines in front of the caves of Acamixtla and that I follow them and the *aquixtle* it sticks me. It is worse than *ortigo,* much worse, and my body was a ball of sores, and when I loosened my rags my flesh bled, because they stuck. I was three days away. And that I go to a stream and that I wash, but where the live flesh was the flies they eat me. And another time I am looking for an ox that lost itself and that I lose my

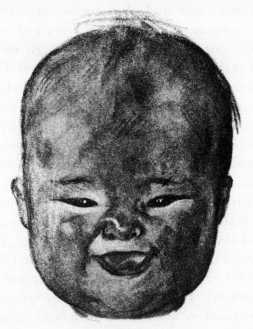

ATANACIO

road. That was in Tierra Fría, toward San Andrés. And that the night falls me and I say better I stay the night here. And I climb in a forked tree and I sleep there covering my head with my small sarape a-la-gallina. There have been many times I sleep like that. And when comes the day passes Don Efren and he says and what and what and that he hits me. Very well! That I keep on looking for the súchil ox and that I find him down by the river and he is in the middle of a tall patch of *acahual*, it is a tall tall weed with burning flowers and I pretend not to see the suchil and he sees me, keeping his head well low and looking at me out of the corner of his little eyes like

DON EFREN

this. And I skirt the whole field so as to get between him and the river and I pick up a heavy stick and zas! — zas! — and that he goes himself. And there he goes, lumbering up the mountainside, back toward San Andrés. Good. But the night catches me. And we are near Chontacuatlán. Then I go toward there, and in the first house there with a little stone wall I stop and I call out if they not have an extra *taco* or a tortilla and that they even collect me the five centavos, that I am full of desire to eat. That I do not eat since the day before. And the señora says come in come in and I go in. But the woman is sick. She has given light to a child only two days back. And she says that look, this little girl is the only one who can give to eat to this family and now take this one tortilla, it is all there is left. But me, how will one tortilla satisfy, and that I remain full of desire to eat. And the señora says look, there is *nixtamal,* but there is no one to grind it unless you yourself grind it. And that I grind the nixtamal. But I was not yet a man. A good lump of the corn I ground on the metate there and the girl child puts the comal on the coals and that she cooks me about ten tortillas, well hot. And that I eat them with salt. And the señora says look, it is impossible that you arrive tonight at San Andres. And I say no, well. And she says throw yourself in the corner where are those corn husks. And that I sleep there, but well. . . . That was now long ago. . . . And there was the revolution. And in the town there were many of the government. But the clarions sounded over by Acapilintla and above by Guadalupe and over on the Huiztteco; and Saavedra came. And the forces of General Saavedra well surrounded the town. The shooting lasted eight hours. And before that was the day when General Salgado, the Zapatista, wanted to take the plaza. And he had cannons and machine guns and he planted over on the next hill,

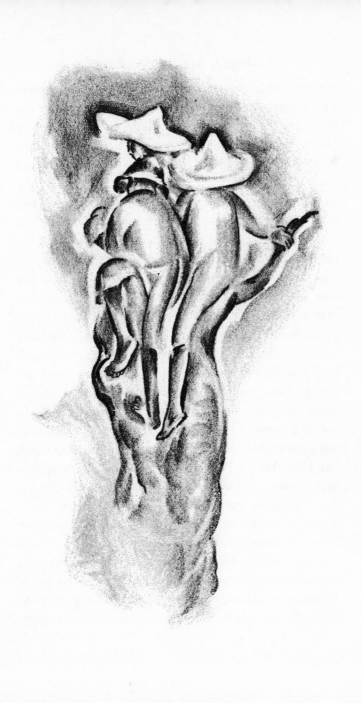

over by Acapilintla itself. But it was the day of Santa Prisca, and when Salgado was ready to fire on the town and he swore he was going to destroy every house, there put themselves white clouds between here and there and he could not. And then arrived the federals and they occupied the plaza and the towers of the *parróquia*. The barranca by my house was full of dead and later the pigs ate their guts. And there was a soldier's woman, a *guacha,* who belonged to Salgado's men, and she had robbed the silver crown from the Virgin of the Light and she was killed. It was when she was climbing the barranca toward Pedro Martin. And came the machine gun fire and she was the only one killed. And the waters came, but what torrents, and her body with her child in her rebozo, she had a baby, and the silver crown and all, was washed eight kilometres away and they found it below Pichagua. . . . My mamá and we, I had a sister, she of the pitted face, were guarding a mine. That is, the mine was closed, but Don Arturo Funter put my mamá there in that little house to guard the picks and shovels. And it was all right, but there was no corn in the town. There had been no crops for two years, so that even if you did have silver you could not buy corn. There was only meat. And there were so many Zapatistas around that the poor could not get out to go to Cuernavaca. But my mamá wrapped our saints, the printed ones, under her rebozo, and she one night crossed the mountains into the state of Morelos and she arrived at Tetecala and there was corn. And with the saints she obtained a good cargo of corn. And we were little bit of ones then and we were very afraid, so we hid under the bed for two days. But then in the dark of the third night came my mamá and we knew it was she because the dog did not bark. And then we had food. And we were little esquintles then. . . . But I had another sister and she was in service. She had been in service precisely in the house of Doña Petra. And the Zapatistas took the cuadrilla of Tehuilotepec. They entered the town at night and being dark men and their clothes all white they quitted their rags and went into the town all naked. And there was little to rob and so they robbed the alcohol from the store of Don Mateos and burned it and then they took the women. When they arrived at our house it was two days later and first they wanted money and then they wanted my sister. And my mother said my sister was not there. But they said yes they knew she was working at Doña Petra's and that my mamá must bring her to the house for them the next night, because they were going to burn the town and kill everybody there and it would be better for my sister to go with them than to suffer. So my mamá said yes. And the next night she hid my sister under the boxes where the hen is setting. And when the Zapatistas come they cannot find her. Nor do they find the *centavos* my mamá has. She has hid them behind a loose adobe in the wall and set the adobe in with the same mud. So they do not find her. But they take our covers from our bed and all our clothes and they leave us all naked. . . . But what I remember most from the Revolution is the hunger, because I was well little.

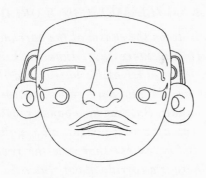

Villa and Zapata were not the only ones. In all the sierras and valleys of Mexico, each region had its own revolutionary hero. Here in Guerrero it was one Augustín Lorenzo. His name is already legend. Don Pancho Cuellar comes down from Ixcateopan and tells me about Augustín Lorenzo. His brother reiterates the discourse. Their father rode with the great caudillo. *That was before the revolution. Things were really bad then. The poor had not even anyone to speak for them. . . . As he talks, Pancho looks as Augustín Lorenzo must have looked. . . . He was pure Indian, from Tlamacuzapa. He made raids on the rich and he was the friend of the poor. Sometimes he made a mistake. But he never robbed. He never robbed — but he interrupted convoys. That is the way Pancho's father joined him. Pancho's father was an arriero and drove burro trains through the mountains, even as Pancho does today. It was different then. There were no automobiles or trucks on the roads; travel was lonely. The road to Tlama-*

*cuzapa leads down the chasm of the barranca toward
Juliantla. It was there that Augustín Lorenzo re-
lieved Pancho's father of his burros and their load.
After that he did not dare return to town, so he
joined the bandit. But was he a bandit? Did he rob?
Señor, he was a revolucionario, all revolucionarios
rob. Even today, except that now the revolution is
finished. There is a corrido about Augustín Lorenzo.
Antonio, Pancho's brother, recites it with gestures.
It is all about the Little Mexican, the Indian, who
went out from his land and gathered his men and
made war on the rich hacendados. The poor people
loved him, and he could come and go in their houses
as he liked. He could even enter the great town of
Iguala and the Federals dared not touch him. And
finally the Carrancistas paid a man; — they took a
poor devil out of jail and they paid him to go and
murder Augustín Lorenzo. And this poor man went
and he joined the forces of the great bandit. And he
became Augustín Lorenzo's close friend. And then
one night he drew his dagger and plunged it to the
hilt in Augustín Lorenzo's back. . . . Afterward
the traitor had to join the army and be sent to Mexico
to save his life. But Augustín Lorenzo bade a sad
farewell to his beloved hills, and sometimes he may
be seen walking in the fields of corn in the valley
there where they buried him, for they say his spirit
does not die.*

Pancho goes on to tell of the fabulous riches that

Augustín Lorenzo stored by, things he hid in the caves in the hills . . . in the Canyon of The Hand, down by Naranjo, they found a hundred saddles with gold and silver embroidery and some elegant charro *clothes with silver buttons, because Augustín Lorenzo loved to dress handsomely, and in that cave he had also hid many little idols and masks of Aztec priests, because Augustín Lorenzo was a Little Mexican, even as are my brother and myself, and he had belief in those things. . . . That is the way Don Pancho Cuellar puts it, and he knows a great deal about those things.*

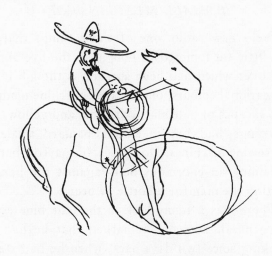

REVOLUCIONARIO

HIS NAME is Jesús Llorado. He is a general without ever having fought battles, a licenciado without ever having studied law, and he has been a congressman without having been voted for. Since he once made speeches in the Revolution and ran errands for Zapata and Obregón, he likes to refer to himself as an incorruptible revolucionario and naturally will always belong to that glorious company. Successful politicians in Mexico must, in the nature of things, be revolutionary.

The first time I ever saw him was in Rafaelito's cantina, the little place that used to be a *pulqueria* until Portes Gil prohibited pulque, but it still has on the outside of it in elegant silver and red letters MEMORIES OF THE. FUTURE. We were listening to

Rafael's new radio, one of those things that look like little tin tombstones bought in the five and ten, and over which had been spread, as though it were the national colours, one of those machine-made Saltillo sarapes of pale blue, dark red, and yellow. . . . A stranger had come in, an old Spaniard, a salesman for sewing machines. Don Jesús, his narrow buttocks sustaining an enormous belly against the bar, was inviting the man for a bottle of beer.

There was a funny look in the pale blue eyes of the general. Someone remarked that he had been drinking since two days back, when he had stepped into the Doña Susanita's little eating place and "borrowed" from her some twenty-two pesos, her total capital. Of course, some say it was two hundred, but that was not true. I know Doña Susana and she herself told me about it; her son, it seems, had been a sympathizer of Luis Cabrera's. But all that is another story.

The old salesman had already asked for a lemonade. He said his stomach was bad. But *mi general* wanted him to drink beer, lots of it. And then he wanted the salesman to tell him things. . . . Why had he come here? What was his nationality? . . . You are a foreigner and you came here to exploit us! Isn't that true? He hardly gave the old fellow time to answer his questions. You are a foreign mule and a *gachupín,* he said. And you came here to make fools of us. Because we are poor and live like *campe-*

sinos you think you can gyp us and get away with it! . . . I know you foreign bastards, all you want is money to take away! The old man was smiling nervously and trying to say he loved this country; that he had his bank account in Mexico (unwise admission), and his family there. By this time Don Jesús' fat and hairy hand had the Spaniard's shirt front and was twisting it, drawing the man closer. The shirt began to tear. On his diminutive behind the general's pearl-handled cannon bulged menacingly. Tell me, he said, reaching for that instrument, tell me in these words, I am as big a bastard as you are!

About this time, my friend, Miguel Maldito, who was running for Presidente Municipal at the time, barged in between the two with loud greetings. He called the general brother, embraced him and invited him for a round of beer all at one and the same time; with the same movement he kicked and pushed the Spaniard toward the door. Whereupon Don Jesús promptly forgot all about his brave defence of *nacionalismo,* and everybody drank, hilariously.

The house of *mi general* is in the second street of the Delights, just two blocks from my own. We frequently pass, greeting each other and lifting our hats. I say, *Buenos dias, mi general!* and he invariably replies, *Buenos dias, ilustre, para servirle!* So we are good friends. Beyond that, we have little to talk about. Except once or twice we have had strange conversations about poetry and, more particularly, about the ineffableness of women. The general is always thinking about them. You can tell that from his political writings.

This house he lives in is a kind of palace. It was formerly the home of a rich merchant whom the Zapatistas turned out. They tore up the floors pretty badly looking for silver and they took care to break everything breakable, like window panes and the saints in their niches. The place has been only partially mended since then, but it serves well enough for Don Jesús as a casual sort of home and office. At the present moment he is the tax collector here and the principal representative of the federal government. Before the revolution the house, which belongs to the nation now, was the residence of the little old Indian priest, the Padre Eulalio of happy memory, the same who, during the religious troubles, was so comfortably taken care of by the rich Doña Petra. Before that, back in colonial times, it was the Custom House during all those years when this was a " free town " and duty was paid on every load of corn or chickens or silver that came into town from outside.

Today they have a better system. There are stamps that have to be put on everything produced, on every receipt for sale of coffee or horses or petates. Don Jesús is the one who sells the stamps. In his custody, too, are all the grand old edifices that once belonged

to the church but are now national property. Like-
wise all receipts from fines collected from the poor
devils luckless enough to get thrown in jail. As a
matter of fact, it is very unsafe for any of the Little
Mexicans who come in from outside and are unknown
here to take a drink in a public place. There is always
the pretext that they were drunk. It is a simple
formula; they spend the night in jail and the following morning must raise the regulation two
peso forty centavo fine to be let free — a fine
which usually cleans them out. Otherwise they sweep
the plaza and repair the stony pavement. The
town is famous among the Indians for this little
recourse.

To be exact, Don Jesús has his fingers in almost
everything around here. It is to him one must apply
for a licence to serenade with a guitar in the streets
at night. That costs twenty-five centavos. Also, any
public procession or religious dance must have his
permission. But if it is a question of a large fiesta
and several groups of half-fanatical indigenous
dancers, Don Jesús does not mix in. Last year, it is
true, he sent a corporal and six soldiers and stopped
a group of *flagelantes* at Easter. Since then they
have those things inside the actual nave of the
parróquia.

Naturally there are many who do not like Don
Jesús. They say that it is with very good reason that
he never leaves his house after dark, not even to go

down to the plaza for a turn as all the neighbours do. They say that during the revolution, when General Salgado threatened the town with his cannons from Acapilintla, Don Jesús retired to the cellar of the Palacio Borda with his family, big pistol and all, and that he took a couple of peons with him who had to stay awake while he slept. But that may be just small-town talk.

What the many among the workers and small tradespeople who depreciate him fail to take into account is that mi general Jesús Llorado is a great poet. This gift has developed with him in making speeches. His public, as a matter of fact, being partly tropical and partly Latin, demands it. They never tire of hearing him refer to the Rising Red Star of the Revolution (they probably would cease to listen if he talked about Economic Stability) and they go into hysterics when he recites for the hundredth time that " Our Clean Sword will shine forth under the Burning Sun of the Struggle . . . until complete happiness reigns in each humble hut and the Immortal Work of the Vindicating Revolution is thrice Blesséd."

From time to time he publishes *manifiestos* sometimes on no provocation whatsoever, simply addressing them to the People. At a glance one might take them for common self propaganda. But they are really much more than that. The last one, which appeared freshly pasted on the colonial planks of Don Jesús' doorway just today, is obviously nothing less than a complete prose poem.

It happens that some small children whom David Siqueiros has been helping and encouraging to paint, are going to show their efforts in the old bakery of the convent of San Bernardino. This new "manifesto" bears simply the name of the town as a title, and dedicates itself (by name) to all the young painters of that group, and "to all the other great artists of the world," with the affection of the said Jesús Llorado, signed "fraternally." And since the general himself called me in and presented me with a copy, and I like it, I proceed to translate:

"Everything in thee is fragrance and greatness; the soul, on feeling the monotonous silence of thy afternoons, remounts its flight toward thy sky, thy sky tinted with burning scarlet, orange, or violet, and it rests there in memory of other similar evenings. . . . Near thee, seen on rainy afternoons, thy seven-million-year-old hills cover themselves with a gas of whitest mist; the Huitzteco, imposing and sublime like all the standards of our patriotic liberties, is caressed by the purest blue the sky contains. . . . In thy heart, historic city, Art Sentiment feels itself palpitate; each house is a true landscape ready-made, full of dreams and poetry, where is heard at each moment the mellifluous and argentiferous voice of thy handsome women, whose agreeable manner awakens the inspiration in the poets, in the painters, in the musicians . . . meanwhile the burnt-red of the ripe fruit of thy coffee groves reminds me of the purple lips of the woman I adore. Where a vision of virgin forests or of jazmin-de-España may be seen through a pleasant window, there one fancies the divine face of the ideal woman, of eyes with sublime expression and of glances indefinable as the infinity, and I can imagine an angel there, with mouth as enervating as opium and as exciting and full of savour as a ripe pomegranate recently opened. . . . My village, thou enlargest my heart during nights full of illusion; thy black nights appear unloosened tresses scattered with crystal drops, thy crystalline fountains are clear mirrors for the portraying of violet sunsets, thy nights silvered by the moon and the miraculous tints of the aurora. . . . Not even the nightingale can explain why the first ar-peggio bursts from its *garganta* . . . nor does the bud of the tuberose understand why, on opening it-self, its perfume is diffused. . . . So it is with the soul of the artist. He does not know the reason for his greatness; the artist feels the Revelation of God in his thoughts and he has for a professor wise Nature herself, from whom he takes his marvellous creations. . . . My town, thy men are hospitable, decent, honourable, unaffected, valiant. . . . Thy women are vases of perfume, lovely angels, charm-ing nymphs, goddesses, true goddesses of Beauty.

. . . In one word, my town, in me thou inspirest Love.

(signed) *fraternally*
Jesús Llorado

Along with the *manifiesto,* which is on a large sheet of pink paper, is printed a juicy black and white woodcut of one of the children, and also, just opposite the woodcut, a photographic portrait of Don Jesús in civilian clothes, hair slicked and an orchid in his buttonhole. It cannot be missed, there on the faded green face of the old building.

The interior of the general's office is as noteworthy as the contents of his *manifiestos.* Entering, you run into a saddle astride an old chair from the convent. Above it, in the corner, is a Victorian hatrack, on which hang: a broad-brimmed black felt hat, congressman style, for visits to the capital; an elegant white sombrero, charro style, nearly a yard across and with horseshoes and eagles embroidered and looped in gold, for processions and fiestas; a well banged-up grey stetson, Texas style, for going places and doing things. On the walls are magazine pictures of Mack Sennett *artistas,* with snapshots of bullfighters inserted from behind, a couple of bas-relief heads of North American Indians with feathers, done in painted plaster, and, just beneath the old lithograph of Hidalgo and the photograph of the governor with his sword, a large photo of a political manifestation in Tecpan-de-Galeana taken some ten years ago in which our Don Jesús is apparently eloquently and successfully addressing half the Indian population of the state of Guerrero. Then there is a big table with printed oilcloth in the centre of the room, with a typewriter, and over it an electric light bulb scantily clothed in thin blue silk embroidered in butterflies, one of those simple little French lampshades that look like someone's lingerie. In a corner of the room are stacked three or four 30-30 rifles.

It just happens that I have a friend in Tecpan-de-Galeana who remembers the visit of General Jesús Llorado and the particular " political meeting " where the big photo was taken. Don Jesús had just started his political career at the time and he had been sent to that little village down on the Pacific to make speeches for someone running for governor and, incidentally, for himself as representative. His party was not popular there in Tierra Caliente, the people being agrarians, and he, for the moment at least, a *carrancista*. Also, he was entirely unknown to them. Add to these conditions the fact that when he arrived he found an enormous religious fiesta in progress. There must have been twenty thousand Indians milling around. My friend says there were about thirty-five groups of dancers and that the plaza was jammed.

Don Jesús, then, was faced with the problem of

starting a political landslide, without any supporters, except the two or three politicians who were with him, and with his public already absorbed in other, more pertinent, business.

However, General Llorado wasted little time. He got several bolts of white cotton, painted them himself with loud and appropriate political sentiments, denouncing agrarianism, and so on (hardly any of these people could read), and had the gigantic posters propped up on poles on the outskirts of the multitude. Then he mounted a barrel and posed and gesticulated most effectively while one of his friends took lots of pictures of him with the enormous crowds filling the foreground.

The pictures later made magnificent newspaper propaganda. In fact General Jesús Llorado practically based his political career on them. But that was just the beginning. Some people say that next year he may be head of the Revolutionary Party in this state.

Jesús Llorado is a person about whom Carleton Beals must have written many times.

Tomado del original que se encuentra
en Taxco de Alarcón, por Guillermo
Spratling, vecino de ese pueblo

PATRON SAINT

Once, while they were building the great church, there came a thunder-storm. It was in 1750 or thereabouts. The Parróquia had reached its final stage and the masons were just carving delicate trivialities of overhanging grotesques and consoles for the crowns of the twin towers. The tall pink structure, with its scaffolding of slender poles bound together with ixtle still encasing it, was like a woven thing thrown up against the darkening sky.

His Señoria, Borda, had gone to Mexico to arrange the purchase of some mines in Guanajuato. The only ones left in charge were the old master of works, the chief mason, and the sculptors.

As the ominous clouds bent low a wind rushed through the streets of Taxco and whistled in the towers. It grew black as night. The maestros, *in great fear, descended the scaffolding. Lightning, in jagged streaks, blasted away across the heights of the Huitzteco. It drew near, as though with deadly intent upon the village and its temple.*

One blazing bolt threw frail towers into dark relief and illumined the glistening dome. The freshly placed majolica letters there read GLORY TO GOD IN THE HIGHEST. . . . *Workmen and villagers gathered in prayer, fearing greatly that the elements of the devil would destroy their beautiful shrine.*

Then suddenly, floating between church-terrace and the heavens, appeared a lovely lady. She was shiningly clothed in voluminous robes of Roman sainthood. Calmly and smilingly, with one hand, she reached forth and detained the flashing bolts of lightning. With the other, holding a palm leaf, she blessed the temple and the inhabitants of Taxco. Then she vanished.

Doña Petra told me about that, but it is well known as a matter of local history. There is a painting of the incident showing the glorious apparition. She was the miraculous Santa Prisca, easily identified by the priests. Little wonder that they enshrined her in the church and made her their patron saint.

DOÑA PETRA

TWO CATHOLIC LADIES

SANTA SEÑORA

IT IS on Sunday morning that Doña Petra Zaragoza transacts her business. Outside her house in the pleasant turmoil of a sunny market few of the townspeople give her a thought or have any idea as to what her business may be. They only see the poor peasants, fathers and sons, big sombreros gripped nervously in front of them, squatting outside or entering her zaguan. Her business concerns lands which lie in a score of remote villages.

The Doña Petra is a capitalist, even though not of the kind interested in stocks and bonds. More properly, she is a Mexican small-town capitalist, typical of the sort who are most fearful of appearance of wealth and spend half their lives in dissimulation of too-evident riches.

She is rarely seen in public and it is probably consciousness of her silver which prevents her walking and talking in the plaza with her neighbours, as all the world does here. When she does sally forth, a solitary figure in folds of voluminous black silk and enveloping rebozo of similar stuff, it is only to step across to the parróquia to confess to the priest or to sit with the Doña Victoria Ybañez and the other old ladies in their special little prayer stalls with their little tin candlesticks and their names all in gilt. There, of course, she is one of the Honourable Guardians of the Sacred Image of the Virgin of Guadalupe.

Her house is the fine old shady one that occupies half one side of the plaza, between the big limestone archangel of the church corner and the pink and yellow front of Borda's palace. It is very dignified and very quiet.

The Doña Petra herself is very dignified and very quiet. Her bearing bespeaks the accumulated importance of seventy years of being rich and also maiden. She is fastidious. When she hires a new servant, for the first six months or so, they say, there is no such thing in her house as a single sweeping of her floors. Two, three, sometimes four times must the poor *pinche* bend her back to the task, and even then the Doña Petra will come along with little hen-clucking sounds and touch the palm of her soft white old hand to the surface just swept and order the creature, usually very young and dark and humble; to repeat the process yet once again.

No one particularly loves the Doña Petra, yet few actually dislike her. The town in general is impressed with her. She is a long-accepted and familiar fact, to be regarded as one regards the ancient and elegant iron *reja* around the atrium of the church, or the inevitable and inscrutable hills above and below town where the silver comes from. But unlike those other local phenomena, one might live in

Taxco for five years and not chance to see the old lady.

Her zaguan is the big blue and white gate, quaintly marbleized, that is between the Botica of Don Miguel Casarrubias and the pulque shop of the Señor Chavarrieta; her first-floor rooms on the street are always well rented for small shops. Within the big gate one glimpses red-tiled and vaulted passageways and the snow-white squat columns and arches beyond which is the compact green of plants in her garden, which is the patio. There are rows of bird cages of split bamboo attached to the walls of this court and in them sing *calandrias* and *tzint-zontles* and *clarines,* birds called by ancient Aztec and Tarascan names, which have voices like exquisite flutes. Serving women are always in and out, busy washing, scrubbing, and interminably cleaning. When they sit in the late afternoons, the Doña Petra has them sew or embroider in order, as she says, that the devil may not perturb their thoughts with passions.

Upstairs the rooms are big and cool and darkened with Victorian plush curtains and lace next the windows. Plants are set along the balconies in the old black pottery they used to make forty years ago at the shrine of Guadalupe. In the corners of this *sala* are tall whatnots of apple and rosewood and in them, behind glass, securely locked, are contained Doña Petra's strangely assorted collection of bibelots. There are some beautiful pieces of old Spanish crystal, carved and gilded, miniature automobiles in silver filigree (1900 epoch), priceless old *talavera-de-puebla* majolica, and the spaces are filled in with modern doll sets of toy china, complete with miniature tin knives and forks. On the walls there are framed diplomas from ladies' societies in the church and several bad paintings of various virgins. And there are four rocking chairs with twisted arms, besides the usual dozen quaint little Mexican straight chairs which have woven bottoms and backs stencilled in gilt and silver indicating their owners' initials. These bear the legend,

NI ME PRESTO NI ME DOY
SOLO DE MI DUEÑA SOY
AVE AVE AVE MARIA!

which means " I " (in this case the chair) " neither lend nor give myself, belonging solely to my owner — ave, ave, etc." Which might have been written about the Doña Petra herself, so apt is it in expressing the sentiments of the mistress of the house.

It is more than twenty years since the old lady has been outside the town. Instead of visiting her properties she has the renters come in to her. No one knows just how much land she possesses, but it is all well scattered in small tracts, and for this reason the agrarians have not been able to confiscate and repartition any of it. In this she has had an enormous advantage over all the big hacendados of the region, who have lived to see their entire system of production supplanted. But then, too, the Doña Petra is a defenceless old woman and a maiden.

The Doña Petra wasted little time in changing the old manner of working which was her uncle's, when he died and left her the property. He was a sort of pioneer and believed in hard work and constructive methods. But she has eliminated all that. She does no planting herself, nor does she send to have it done; neither does she construct houses, though she always has a little lime or adobe or a few hundred tiles on hand to sell when offered a good price. The thing that most profoundly interests the Doña Petra is what the yearly rental of the lands is going to bring her in good hard pesos, and that they in turn continue to multiply. Also she enjoys hearing her servants refer to her as the *santa señora*. And she attends mass regularly.

The Doña Petra does not invest her silver, nor does she entrust it to the Banco de México. She is a sort of small banking institution in herself. She lends money and receives good security for it in land. Anyone may borrow money from her with the sole security of good land. Her interest rate is twenty to forty per cent a month, which is not uncommonly high in these parts.

Not since she was a young woman has the Doña

Petra been in person to one of her villages. True, these trips are tiresome for a woman, but she has had her properties now nearly a lifetime and there are still people who can recall her regular visits to far off haciendas. Some people wonder how she can even remember which tract of land she is renting and which lies fallow. But the fact is that she does know and she does remember the boundaries of her well-watered fields in Cacalotenango and she even remembers the long tortuous path to Juliantla and Tlamacuzapa.

It was along that same road, a long time ago, that something occurred that properly belongs to the old lady's private history. Not that there was any scandal, and it may even be that the story is not true. However, knowing the Doña Petra and her countrymen, I suspect that it is true, and, anyway, I feel that if the details are a bit vague and inaccurate, something of a similar nature must surely have happened to her which would not be difficult to imagine.

She was very good-looking in those days, according to the old coloniales. She had smooth cheeks and firm legs and she rode horseback English-lady style when out inspecting her properties. She was infinitely more direct in dealing with her countrymen than she is now. She would pause on her trips to pass a word in greeting with all the small farmers and landowners over there.

No one will ever know in how many good Mexican hearts she stirred passions. After all, how could they resist her strange blonde attractions when the only women they had known were all dark? Certain it is that no such thoughts passed through the mind of the Doña Petra. In her generation, Spanish traditions still held. And even though she were Mexican, it had not yet become fashionable to admit, much less to exult in, a few drops of Indian blood. As for the Indian race itself, it existed only to work and produce for the class to which she belonged.

One day in passing on her way to Tlamacuzapa — it was at the crossing of a small stream where she invariably stopped to water. her horses — she found, thrust in the fork of an ahuehuete tree, at eye level, a little flat rock scribbled on. It said merely SEÑORITA, and there was a flaming heart. The Doña Petra smiled, but took no further note of the thing.

Some fellow from the hills there was anxious to become her *novio,* to be her lover. Since not even the Doña Petra herself ever knew him, his name remains unknown. It requires but slight effort to imagine what he was like. He probably worked a small milpa or ranch. He wore huaraches on his feet and a broad sombrero, given a certain style by the curve of its brim; on horseback he fastened it with a handwoven band of horsehair dangling under his jaw. His calzones were of white cotton and his shirt pink, maybe lavender. He belonged to that class of Mexicans whose faces are like Aztec masks, beardless, dark, like fine bronze. He had black, mysterious and childishly observant eyes. From time to time the dignity of his face would relax into a flashing smile, revealing incredibly white teeth and frank good humour.

He considered himself the equal of any *catrín*, as the mountain people like to refer to people who wear town clothes.

There were no results from the first note so the boy wrote another.

The next time she passed this way recollection of the little scribbled stone flashed back to the Doña

Petra. As she approached the spot she glanced toward the ahuehuete and there in the fork was another smooth flat rock. This time it was written all over, but nearly illegible, because the words had been merely scratched on the surface with another pointed rock. So the Doña Petra, with a mild access of curiosity, took the little slab of rock and put it in her saddlebag. She probably thought no more of it until she was back in her house in Taxco that night. Then she got it out and with difficulty deciphered it. It said, in gravely smooth Spanish:

SEÑORITA SINCE THE HAPPY MOMENT IN WHICH I FIRST SAW YOU I HAVE FELT AN ARDENT DESIRE FOR YOUR PERSON GOD GRANTING AND WITH THE AID OF SAINT PETER AND SAINT PAUL MAY THE DAY BE NOT LONG DELAYED WHEN YOUR BODY BE JOINED WITH MY BODY

One may only conjecture what may have been the Doña Petra's immediate reaction to this love note which did not speak of love. Certainly that night she broke the thin slab of stone in small pieces and scattered them. Perhaps it was no problem for her at all. The boy's note was serious enough, but it concerned earthy, basic matters and those things had never entered into the Doña Petra's scheme of things. She had never been — nor did she intend to be — in contact with the soil.

About that time, so they say, the Doña Petra ceased altogether to make trips to her villages. No one ever knew if there was a reason for this. However, she has often been heard to remark, even as she has remarked to me, that the Inditos — as she calls all descendants of the Aztecs — are all right seen in town, but that out there in their villages they are *muy naturales!* — indicating, as though there were a grave moral attached, that these little Mexicans are not only primitive but are given to " natural impulses."

VIRGEN DE LA LUZ

Greater, more colourful masses of flowers are carried to the little chapel of the Virgen de la Luz than to any other of the town's eleven shrines. Purple, white, and green orchids, *clavelin* in heavily odorous, thickly strung chains, *rosal, flor-de-los-muertos,* armfuls of lilies find their way there from far places. They enter by many and devious routes, including the twisting little passage dominated by the mass of the parroquia which is called in Aztec " Little Street of the Land of the Gods." Following that direction one finds the Virgin. To see her place and her people is to understand what has happened to religion in Mexico.

MARÍA-DE-LA-LUZ

This shrine has that feeling of being at once simple, inscrutable, and vastly significant.

The image of the Virgin is a small chromo print, darkly stained and without glass. Even with the sun at mid-day outside it is obscure in the gloom, even less distinguishable for the matted accumulation of gold and silver *milagros* with which it is framed to the extent of several feet. This chapel is not a part of the Catholic church, neither does it pay taxes as belonging to its holy dueña, the venerable Doña María. It is something very special and apart.

Her shrine is particularly sacred to the Indians. They travel long distances, coming down from the mountains or up from the hot country below Taxco. Thousands come all unannounced and they bring tribute. The Virgin is worshipped unquestioningly by these dark, unemphatically moving people who decorously supplicate alleviation or who come to render thanks for favours received. She is a most powerful virgin and renowned for countless miracles. Hundreds of votive offerings, painted *retablos,* hung on the adobe walls of her humble chapel attest her willingness to oblige.

As in all the houses of the poor, there are no windows to her shrine. Only a door. It is so dark one must have a candle to make out the retablos. In one corner, the same colour as the sombre walls, sits the Doña María, piously, gravely squinting, occasionally scattering pecking chickens with a movement of her cane. There are many animals. Chickens mingle with cats and outside are roped mongrel dogs which snap at one's back. The entrance is dusty. There is nothing elegant or pretentious here.

The old woman, the Doña María, looks incredibly wise. Not merely wise but shrewd and cunning. Sitting there in her dingy gown she piously prays, interceding, with lengthy, placating words, for the benefit of a barefoot mother in rebozo who kneels with her home-made candle of brown tallow in front of the obscure chromo Virgin; or, as I myself saw and heard there one morning, she accepts a gold coin from a poor Indian and his young son, telling them as they stand there humbly with battered sombreros in their hands, that they must also bring oil. " *Eso es* " — oil is the thing!

Her role is more than that of priest, she is both intercessor and oracle. There is much more here than meets the eye. From where does the Doña María derive and how has she, a woman, achieved her holy office of priestess among a presumably Catholic people? One day she told me, in the same half-persecuted, pious voice with which the Doña Petra also speaks, that she has not been outside the house for twenty-five years — not since her holy mother died. Perhaps the chapel is an inheritance.

Socially, of course, she has no place in Taxco, no more than has the holy Niño Fidencio in Guadalajara. She is not of the people, she is of a world apart.

And she is distantly removed from the conventional religious formula of the Mexican bourgeoisie. She is Taxqueña and she is mestiza; but her lot has been thrown with the Indians of pure blood, the *campesinos,* on whom depend her office and her sustenance. And she is well connected. Don Blas, the sacristan of the parroquia, claims cousinship. His daughter is named María-de-la-Luz for her shrine. And she is an aunt of the Señorita Otilia, she of the cantina on the corner. Otilia would probably not advertise the fact, being at that ugly stage of social development where one tries to forget Indian tradition in order to become *gente decente*. It is a process akin to " crossing the line " among the habitants of Harlem. Neither extreme is bad, but the middle stage is one of presumption and a bad mixture of native with bourgeois taste. The women begin by treating their hair and using cosmetics, which are never quite right with brown skin. Men of this class, as a first evidence of the new order, leave off their gracious, comfortable huaraches for bulbous, shiny shoes, in which they can no longer walk with the quiet unpretentious movement of their race.

But the Little Indians who worship at the shrine of the Virgen de la Luz approach her with an immaculate simplicity. They are continuing, in all innocence, a religious impulse which certainly antedates the conquest, which is probably older than the Catholic church. They are the same people who have idols from the graves of their ancestors placed to guard their corn, who set up an image of Tonantzin, goddess of fertility, for the success of their crops. They call these idols of polished, finely carved green and black stone, *chanes* — spirits. The efficiency of these spirits acquires such fame that, among a community, they are frequently rented out for the season. In Huahuastla, in Titzicapán, in Tetipac these things exist. To these people it is no secret that for her service Tonantzin requires oil. . . . But more of that later.

All over Mexico these shrines exist. Presumably they are private chapels about each of which has grown an aura of faith in the miraculous. It is a strange compromise between an imposed religion and embedded tradition. With the weakening of social and economic power of the orthodox church their popularity increases. They seize the imagination of the poor, providing a sense of intimacy, of proximity to the Source. And their ideology unconsciously gravitates to that which is, after all, Aztec.

That the keepers of these shrines are more or less venal goes without saying. Their stock in trade, in the form of milagros or precious metals and of painted retablos, which attest marvellous cures, or rescues from bandits (or of bandits from federals) or immunity from the bite of a serpent or alacrán, is incontrovertible evidence of supernatural and desirable aid. Their testimony is more effective than guide-book recommendations. The shrines may be frequently brazen inventions, becoming veritable gold mines for their owners. A fancied apparition of a cross on the floor, an unexpected recovery, or a dream like a visitation, provide basis for origin and capitalization.

The actual origin of the Doña María's shrine to the Virgen de la Luz is a mystery. No one can remember the circumstances of the event. Her power increases day by day. But in this unspacious adobe shack, sombre with votive offerings, its floor of earth pressed by countless Indian knees, amidst an atmosphere thick with the odour of the Aztec flor-de-la-muerte and impure with the person of the revered Doña María and her horde of cats, Tonantzin, Mother of the Gods, still lives and is well adored.

We wander out into the translucent night, pausing to contemplate the mysterious black of laurel in shadow. The plaza is deserted now. Someone suggests a serenade. Then Marihuana. We can smoke it over back of the convent, or on top of it. We will get the Bun to come along, with his guitar. The night is quiescent and caressing. It will be a good time to sing Las Mañanitas. . . . The ruined patios of the old convent stink. Neighbours have come here daily for too many years now. . . . Just beside a fallen vault the jagged wall-end gives foothold. The Chicken goes first, followed by the Clay Man. Seen over flying buttresses the arch of the night comes close. The Siren brings a bottle of mezcal. The Chicken carries in his blouse a few lumps of panochita. *He says the weed is gilded that much quicker with the sweet.*

We are above the town, will soon be above Mexico. We sit there in the operatic balcony of the ruined tower, silently smoking. . . . A rapid pull, then deep, filling the lungs with the gentle stuff and holding it. No smoke comes forth, only pallid air. . . . The effect crystallizes. There is no novelty, but the Siren giggles. Something the Chicken said. It wasn't funny. But it was so funny. The Siren is doubled up with mirth. Giggles and giggles. He is exhausted . . . another fag of the Doña Marihuana. The Bun appears over the parapet. He has his guitar. Then the Duck. Another round. . . . The mountain is a picture postcard, tangible, here by one's side. There are only two dimensions and I could pass my hand over the dome of the cathedral. What thoughts! Why we are here no one knows. But it's funny. It's incredibly funny. The Bun is singing. His voice and he are separate and distinct. How marvellous! You can see his voice. Or at least you can feel it. How lightning-like is the brain! We were talking. But what about. The Clay Man only smiles over there. His arm is back of the Chicken. The Siren is sad. He says he is only a poor unhappy one, will always be. An enormous black wave engulfs him. He is filled with Weltschmerz. Where did I get the word? Anyway, it was that. What was I thinking at the moment? It was unimportant but crucial. I am explaining, certainly. Now all is clear. Super-clear. I am talking, talking, talking, talking, and then all is clear.

The Siren, poor fellow, is weeping tragically. If we could only see what sadness, what unearthly sadness, there is in the world. I could step over the dome of the cathedral. . . . But we must have a plan. . . . The Bun is no longer singing. He says he is a parrot. He is talking like one. That's the way they talk, he is saying. He is on the edge of the parapet with his back that way. I pull him here. He climbs a little way up the pillar of the tower. It is terribly funny. Lorito ! — Loro ! *he is saying.* Soy loro, *he clucks. His heels are on the ledge and he hangs downward by one claw. He may be, he may be a parrot.* Lor-r-r-r-ro ! *he squawks.* Bread for Polly ! Bread for Polly ! *This is better than drinking, no dizziness. It is much nicer and you can think so fine.* Dame la pata ! *says the Chicken.* Give me your hand, Polly, *he is saying. Come. Come, give me your hand. The parrot, the Bun, squawks, shrills, reaches beak for shoulder of the Chicken, grasping in space for the finger of the Chicken. Then he is on the stone, right here at our feet. His head bleeds blood. He is talking about God as he gets up. God-is-love! God-is-love! He still sounds like a parrot. Six inches and he would have landed in the plaza below. What thing is this? Or are we all dreaming? The Siren says let's get some water. With water comes the third dimension. . . . In one swallow of water there is reality. We drink.*

MEXICAN ARTIST

PEOPLE here in the town would never think of calling him " artista." They refer to him as " Maestro," which is more inclusive, a mark of recognition. It is like the title " Don," which, since the revolution, is applied to all those who these people think deserve respect. It is a subtle distinction. There are a lot of well-dressed people who neither merit " Don " nor " Maestro." You have to understand to just whom it should be applied. There is no rule about it, and there is no college which can make a " Don " of anybody. Thus, it is always the " Maestro " Ayala, though Angel is a poor Indian with a terribly patched pink shirt and faded overalls and he wears huaraches. Even the rich Doña Petra and the doctor, Don Antonino, speak to him as Maestro. For the skill which he has in his hands he is as well known in Iguala and Huitztac as he is in this town where he was born.

Clients come to him from ten leagues away. For every miracle that occurs in the lives of the faithful it is almost certain that Angel Ayala will be painting a record of it, a retablo to be presented to their patron saint. Besides doing these things for the religious, his services are also in great demand as a painter of cards and tablets for the gamblers of loteria. He is also the best maker of masks for the religious fiestas in these parts, a thing for which he is probably more famous among the Little Mexicans than for any other of his talents. Further, he writes letters for the many who are not learned — love notes are a specialty — and on Sunday nights he plays the bass viol in the serenade in the plaza. . . . The life of Angel Ayala is intimate and integral with that of the town. He is indispensable, which is more than is to be said for most small-town artists, outside of Mexico.

Angel lives just below my house in one room with a dirt floor. There are no windows, only a door. Just inside the door, sits Angel on a little low seat which he made himself, working in the only lighted part of his home. You can see him there from the balcony. In the obscurity of his background you can make out the figure of his wife, Rita, colour of dusty chocolate, and until recently you could see three or

DON ANGEL AYALA

four very small children of various tones of the same colour.

There were four, to be exact. But only a short time ago there were three deaths in that little family. It came about very casually, as those things always do in Mexico. No one thought of a doctor, though some old woman came and made a " tea " for the sick children, and of course they kept the door shut

tight so that the " air might not hit them." It was a fever, probably what is called *sarampión*. The children didn't last long. The three died within two days. The last to go was the one called Angelito, named for his father.

Rita has it in her head that Angel is the one to blame. It happens that there was the complication of a new sweetheart in Angel's life. Her name was Guadalupe. At any rate, Rita claims that Angel neglected doing anything about the children for thinking about his Lupita, that he spent the time as in a trance, thinking about the girl or composing notes to her; that at nights he went with his friends to play *gallos* beneath her window. The situation was still worse, because Angel was already having difficulties

with a third, a woman he had been keeping over in the low neighbourhood of San Miguel. . . . I know, because Angel himself had just come to sell me a retablo a client had left on his hands, and he told me all about the affair. Rita knew, too, but like most of her countrywomen, she had long ago resigned herself to a silent acceptance of whatever might be her husband's love interest of the moment. But her resignation had been scattered by this business of the sarampión and the death of three of her children.

But for Angel there were further complications. This time artistic as well as emotional. He had promised some Indians in Tizicapan to make them a new Santiago. The old one in their chapel had become entirely worm-eaten, being a relic of the sixteenth century. Angel had been charmed with the commission.

It is well known that for a good Santiago there are two prime requisites, a white horse, and long curling locks for the Saint himself. And Santiago can possibly do without the horse, but the curling locks are indispensable. The Maestro had been working on this, lavishing all his attention, all his craft on it, for a long time. The horse was done, had been shown to all the neighbours. He was carved in zompantle and covered with white lacquer. True, his knees bent the wrong way, but it rather added to his Early Christian expression.

Angel was very enthusiastic. He had the wood for the Saint's limbs all put aside and he had already bought nice blue glass eyes for him. The thing he was waiting for — would have had to wait for perhaps only another month or so — was the question of the curly locks. For that, he had been counting on An-

gelito. For that reason he had never cut his hair.
When the child died, the locks were just reaching his
little brown shoulders, black and glistening, almost
purple, and fine, like the silk from Chilapa.

Now Angel is desolate. He lacks heart for anything, even for the figure of Santiago. And Rita has
been treating him very badly about the new sweetheart. The other has thrown him out completely and
taken up with the judge's clerk. He has not made a
centavo since the children died. Even then he had
to borrow the five pesos with which to pay for each
little burial. He explained it all to me yesterday. He
speaks quite simply about it, with no hint of com-
plaint. Everyone in town knows what has happened
in his house. However, this morning I saw him working there in his doorway and he was making buzzard
masks. There were six or eight of them under way.
He told me, and he even smiled as he said it, that the
fiesta of the Chapel of Guadalupe was only eight
days off; that those from Tecalpulco were offering
the Virgin a tiger dance. And for the tiger dance
he had made masks ever since he could remember. It
was almost a part of his life.

He came up to my house and we had a long talk.
He promised to borrow an old manuscript of the
dance for me. I could think of nothing better than
to lend him a picture book. He had wanted to see
pictures of Americanos. I selected a volume of Peter
Arno's caricatures. The Maestro took it very seri-

ously. He said that Mr. Arno must be one of these
"hurried" artists. But when he came to the one
about the eunuchs, he could scarcely contain himself.

He sat quietly enjoying it.

"You like it?" I asked.

"Sí, sí," he said. "With their big pants they look
just like the *touristas.*"

Music in the night. Over in the house with the bananas and papayas, back of white pillars in the moonlight, they are practising. It must be practice, because there is a sort of melancholic repetition. And the flute always makes the same equivocation. I am listening in the garden. This music in any other place would cause a general protest. Here, at this distance, it is all right. It is fitting and quaint. The piece they are playing was once a waltz. It will be ready to be played in the plaza about two weeks from next Sunday. They have three other pieces, which include

Sonny Boy, Negra Mala, and the thing they always play for bull fights. But they are all equally sad. Especially if they have to play them in the church or beneath windows on nights like this.

The strains continue unrelentingly, making a thousand new beginnings, far into the night. The sound of the guitars is like wind in the trees and the flute and bass viol strain and pull with coaxing insistence. I finally go into the house.

Then they are by the fountain beyond the gate and someone is singing there. This is something different. There are three and one of them is singing the Papaganga. It is something Tarascan, rich and full of mystery. The serenade is for the wife of the postmaster. Don Epifanio must be away. There is no sound from the house, only the shutters have been gently opened a little. Music in the night does that. It opens something. After a while, they will move over by the plaza and do the same for Lolita and Susanita, interrupting sleep with something sweeter, more ardent than sleep. It moves with decorum, that music. But it stirs and brings to life something deep down. It is a formula, of course, but they do not know that. Neither do they know that what some negro sings in London, or what Mr. Coward composes, is more fashionable this year. . . . Perhaps Angel, who is one of the silently enamoured ones, will tell me of a new conquest tomorrow.

TATA LUIS

OF THE OLD REGIME

HE MUST have been nearly ninety. His mind harked back to the time of Carlota and Maximiliano and to the days when he was a child selling mangoes in the plaza. His job was more a matter of tradition than anything else. No one ever expected him to be exact. As a matter of fact, the tolling of the hours after eleven o'clock in the morning meant nothing. They were merely a pleasant sound, because Tata Luis, about eleven, had found his buddy, old Timoteo, and together they had gone for their morning cup of mezcal. From then on, they were in and out of the cantina, arguing and drooling and gesticulating. When he happened to think of it, Tata Luis went off to the tower and his bells, where, filled with a sense of high duty, he pulled heartily on the old ropes. It was not unusual for two o'clock to be rung three times and four o'clock was apt to be sounded thirteen o'clock. By three o'clock, he was on his way up the hill to his home and family and you could hear him all the way to Guadalupe if he happened to be in the mood for advising the neighbours. This was an almost daily occurrence and his querulous old voice, attempting to bellow at people, gave vent to all his most personal opinions about the world in general and his neighbours' wives in particular. Tata Luis, as he used to say himself, was as full of stories as a dog is of fleas. He would grasp my hand earnestly, telling me that he had much to talk to me about. Only what he had to tell were not stories, but endless chronicles. For him, the church was still the only institution in Mexico. Politics and government and education were just so much applied ornament.

We were in the bell tower one day and he waved his hand toward Tierra Caliente. In his day, he would say, the church was master of all the land, it needed no one's charity. Over there, he said, as far as you can see, all that was property of the church. And here below us, all the grand houses you see within a block of this church, all of them were of the church. What did the people do for land? I asked, ingenuously. Why, they paid a sort of gratification to the church, he said. And the church paid all its workers. Not like it is today. Everyone had some duty to

the church. Some kept books, there were the sacris-
tans, the choir-singers, the organist, even the official
dog-runner. Yes, they had a *perrero,* whose office it
was to keep the dogs off the church steps. He even
had his holy uniform and a long whip. In the evenings he had to go through the cemetery, running out
the dogs. Otherwise, they would dig up and eat the
corpses of the recently buried. The workers were all
paid.

Yes, he continued, they were all paid. But that
didn't keep them from claiming property of the
church in payment for salary, when Juarez came to
sell the church's lands. There was Juan Mollano, the
first sacristan. He kept that palace there by the
plaza, which is now the jail. And Lorenzo Adán, he
of the organ, he passed three houses on to his family.
They all belonged to the church. It was that way
with the uncle of Doña Petra Zaragoza. He had
never had anything before. . . .

But my brother, he would never take anything.
He was bell-ringer for thirty-five years. He died.
Yes, he died, and he passed the job on to me. And
the church has always paid us. It was a peso twenty-
five centavos a week. Now they pay me one fifty —
and don't think it wasn't hard work to get it. I had
to beg for it and I even threatened to turn in my keys.
For what can one do with one twenty-five a week
these days.

His talk, like his life, was full of simple and profound incident, without any glory or any particular plot. He could have written an intimate history of Mexico since the days of the great liberator, but he could not even read. His face preserved the features of his land, of the rude cliffs of the Huitzteco and the hidden beauties of strange plants, like thoughts, in the interstices.

He lived through the thirty odd years of Díaz' reign without ever forgetting that he himself was a *religioso,* that this Don Porfirio was an outsider. It was as though it were just yesterday that Díaz and his army were arriving on top of the hill above town, asking permission to come in. He was in flight, coming down from Toluca, just beginning his amazing campaign, the same that finished in Oaxaca far to the south. Yes, he said, Don Porfirio had seventeen thousand men, but he sent his ambassadors to beg permission to enter this town. And then there was a council and Marcos Toledo, who was commandant then, sent him word that they were welcome to stay the night, but that they must pass on the next day. Díaz thought it was an ambush, so he waited. And it was nine o'clock and then it was ten o'clock and they had not come down. So Marcos took thirty men from his guard and went up the hill and talked to Porfirio Díaz, to tell him that they could come through. But Díaz disarmed him and his thirty men and he put them in the files under guard, and then he came down to occupy the plaza. He was here three days and there was fighting all the time. It took him that long to get forty-five men out of the towers of the parroquia. And each day they killed cattle for food, until there was none left in all the town. But Díaz lost six thousand men in those three days and he used up all his arms and ammunition. And when it was over he wanted to see the dead among the townspeople. But there were none. No, señor, there were no dead. . . . But yes, there was, there was one. He had his brains blown out by a cannon when he tried to get some mezcal from his house one night. (Tata Luis' statistics, as may be seen, always fitted the occasion.) When Porfirio Díaz left the town he conscripted every male inhabitant above twelve years of age. Yes, I was with them, and so were my three brothers. The rays of the sun poured down on us and there were many who fell and had to be carried. In one day we marched all the way to Tepecuacuilco in Tierra Caliente. Before arriving at Zumpango we brothers managed to get away. We would wrap our heads in our sarapes and simply walk off into the night. How well I remember that after walking all night, I climbed into the tall greenness of an *amate* tree and I tied myself there with rope. Yes, they say that Porfirio Díaz with that army went all the way to Tehuantepec. He passed by Tlapa and Huahuapam. And then Juarez died and Porfirio was President. But he never came back to this town. We never loved him here. Though he used to say that he would give ten soldiers of his army for one from here. . . .

But I remember much more than that. When I was just a *chamaco* there was Maximiliano and Carlota. They came down in their coach one time and, because my grandfather was the oldest man in town — he was a hundred and sixteen — they gave him a premium of silver. And I remember my father's brother. He was married to four women at the same time. He was truly a man. And he was chief of the plaza in Iguala. And just because he tried to help the other side with a little ammunition, they were going to shoot him. But his wife, his new one, came and she said to them, let me pay you not to kill him. And they laughed at her and they said, how do we know you can pay for him and besides how do we know what he is worth. So she said do not worry, you put him in the scales and weigh him equally with the silver I will bring. And it was much, much silver, because he was a man with a heavy shadow. . . . But he had had part in many revolutions. And just before that time he had been helping my general Salgado make silver pesos. That was here in the town and they coined them in the house where Don Jesús Llorado lives now. The silver they lifted from the mines at Xitinga and Atlixtac. Yes, they were badly made, but the silver in them was good, it had much gold along with it. And they were bigger than the federal pesos.

Tata Luis paused. The invitation was for a little drink — meaning would I lend him the wherewithal. He came in and we sat down to a bottle of Habanero. *Ay, que bueno!* he said, this must be cognac. Any liquor other than mezcal would be cognac. And this was certainly fine. He talked about the wine they used to have in the church. The sacristan was always " lending " him a pull on the bottle. But what a sacristan! It seems there was something between Father Lupe, the priest, and that man's wife. The sacristan always had wine, and sometimes he sold it in Iguala, but no one thought anything of it. The Father once tried to find out where his wine went. He called everyone to solemn confession. But no one could tell him anything about it. Then he remembered that the sacristan had not confessed in a long time and he said, My dear Eulalio, for the good of your soul come and confess. All right! They went to the confessional stall, the Father in his little box and Eulalio outside. The Father listened to all the sacristan had to say and then he said from his side of the grill, but my son have you never taken wine from the church? The sacristan said, I cannot hear, Father, what you are saying. I asked, said the Father, if you have never taken wine from the church. I still cannot hear you, Father, says the sacristan. So the priest said, that is strange, let us change places, so that I may see for myself what is the matter. So they changed places and the Father said, now tell me again, my son, what you said. And the sacristan said, when did you last see my wife, Father? And then the Father said, Truly, one cannot hear. So the sacristan received the Father's blessing and went about his business. Tata Luis said that there was always plenty in the family of the sacristan. God, he said, gives to those he loves.

He always spoke of serving God in the parroquia, but he admitted that God moves about, from one church to another. He said that the most powerful saint in the town was the Nuestro Señor in the little church of the Holy True Cross. That he was famous all the way to the Pacific and over into the state of Morelos. Once, over in Acuitlapán, there was such a drouth as never had been before. The Acuitlapeños begged for the loan of the Nuestro Señor, and six men carried him there on their backs. It was a two day trip over the mountains, but no sooner were they there than the rain came down in torrents. Truly, it was miraculous. But then, afterward, the Acuitlapeños wanted to keep the saint in their church, and there was fighting, but finally the men from our town carried him off triumphantly. There were no casualties among them, but among the Acuitlapeños there were three men killed and a señora with a black eye. After that, they always called him the Little General.

Again and again had the Little General been brought forth in procession so that the rains might

come, and every time had there been a good down-
pour. Just last year, he said, as we brought him out
from his shrine, there appeared a tiny cloud over the
highest peak of the Huitzteco. We took him over
to the church of San Miguel and from there to the
chapel of the Ojeda and by the time we had reached
the neighbourhood of the White Cross there was
thunder and the clouds had joined themselves in dark
array. And as we were passing the convent, it was al-

ready raining on both sides of the town. What was
truly a miracle was that the waters fell copiously on
every hand, except in the direction of the shrine of
Nuestro Señor and there they left a narrow pass,
quite dry, for his return. And though the waters fell
we were not wet.

He said the Virgin of Guadalupe was strangely
eccentric about bringing the waters, that once she
almost washed the town away with a cloudburst
when they had taken her in a procession. After that,

he said, grinning, we brought out the Child Jesus when we wanted rain. That was so he could show his holy mother a thing or two!

His funeral was just at dusk. I had been off in the hills and as I approached the town I could see the flares of pitch-pine as the little single file of mourners rounded the knob of a hill this side of his house. There were three pieces of music, a violin, a bass viol and a flute, and they were playing some old-fashioned waltz. It was sad enough. As darkness crept over the scene it became a little weird. By the time I had reached the plaza they were already there. The coffin was resting on the cobbles, outside Rafael's cantina, and the women were grouped silently together. They looked as though they had been used to waiting for such things all their lives, standing there with black rebozos enveloping head and arms and shoulders in a single gesture and with one hand pressing the black folds of the garment across the lower half of their faces. The ancient Doña Clotilde, she who had borne Tata Luis so many children, who had quieted him so many times when he had returned drunk and shouting from this same little cantina, sat huddled on the stones of the pavement, her two arms covering her face and head. Not a sound came from her.

The coffin was very large and splendid, I thought,

for the remains of one so poor and shrivelled as Tata Luis. It was of beautifully varnished red cedar.

As I returned to the plaza again after supper the cortège was just getting under way. Old Timoteo and his three companions came out from the cantina and very solemnly, staggering slightly, but not under the weight of Tata Luis, raised the coffin to their shoulders. The music struck up Sonny Boy and they were off to the Holy Field to bury him. The single file of women and children followed the coffin and the music and then came the rest of us. People in the street stopped to listen ceremoniously and raised sombreros from their heads, as a matter of course, as the coffin passed in front of them. There were two more stops for rest. Both times — it may have been by accident — the coffin was set down in front of a cantina. The pall-bearers and their friends sought liquid solace. Timoteo came forth from the last with a large bottle of mezcal sagging his coat pocket. . . . I recalled the story that it was this same Timoteo who, during the revolution, when Tata Luis was carried off bound to a burro by the Zapatistas to be executed, followed him and begged to be allowed to kiss his friend good-bye, and that he embraced him and kissed him on the mouth, passing him by that means a small knife. And that Tata Luis then managed to cut the cords with it and that he rolled over the cliff at Aguatitlan, escaping with his life.

At the burial ground, the coffin, shiny and resplendent in the light of the pine torches, was set down and opened, the slender little old body which only partly filled it was taken out and wrapped in an old sarape and lowered without further ceremony to its final rest. . . . The coffin, it seems, belonged to the sacristan, who keeps it there in the church for this purpose, renting it for two pesos a burial, providing it is returned the same day and in good condition.

So we left Tata Luis, a servant of the church and of the old regime, one who had never presumed. He appeared no more formal in the wrappings of his old sarape than he had actually been in life.

Angel slyly calls them the syncronizados. *He sees them as they arrive in the plaza and get out of their cars, which were hired at the Regis or the Ritz. They stop to consult their watches before looking at the church. This obedience to Time seems to him incredibly funny, particularly when instead of sitting down on those nice benches in the plaza or looking about, they continue standing there for twenty minutes heatedly discussing whether they shall leave at two or at two-thirty. He does not realize that these people never enter into a country, that they merely travel.*

They have finally entered the church. There are exclamations of "What a waste of gold!" — "Do you think these natives appreciate it?" — "Now, Mr. Terry says this baroque is not pure," and they shortly emerge asking their small-boy guide what else one should see in the town, without even glancing around. They are full of disappointment that the "natives" do not wear breech clouts. They insistently refer to all the things in the market as "native" — never just Mexican. Of course by this they mean the things or people one examines at a place called a resort. And this not yet being a resort country, things puzzle rather than interest them. It is difficult for them to enjoy. One must maintain a casual air toward anything indigenous. Why go to a foreign country, particularly one where nearly everyone is poor, if one cannot patronize? Shown a dance mask of fine yellow lacquer made for last week's fiesta, the expression is, " How funny! " or, " Queah, isn't it? " And in order to be amusing the streets of the town must be identified with " Main Street," the little hotel is the " Ritz," and so on. . . . But these Americanos are not the only tourists. Many Spaniards and others who call themselves Mexican are just good tourists pretending to be residents of the country. Like those who come and ecstasize and, with unbounded but pointless enthusiasm, liken the town to Toledo. And like Don Máximo, who warns me that talking with the Indians will corrupt my Spanish. Cortes, I suppose, must have been the first tourist in these parts. . . . They all have much in common, even the lady and gentlemen watercolourists and Richard Halliburton. . . . No, the tourists, no matter how fervid, rarely arrive at Mexico. Angel is within his right when he likens them to the synchronized sound movies, which have captions in Spanish and motivations and reactions which reject reality.

LOLA

LOLA

THE LADY writer was disturbed about them. What, she said, have they to live for? Their life is a drudge. They cannot even enjoy pretty clothes. Look at them work. That stone thing in the kitchen, the thing they grind the corn on, is a symbol of slavery. And the symbol of their womanhood is that drab scarf you call the rebozo. Their very shape enveloped in it becomes one of self-abnegation.

I look at them, she continued, and wonder. The young ones, yes, they are beautiful: like flowers, delicate-featured and modest. But they become mature so soon. What does it? It can't be just work.

I pointed out that even without a Junior League to attend, they really lived very full lives. I tried to

say something about the business of living and func-
tioning within racial traditions, but it was somehow hard to make clear.

She went on, remarking that what they needed
was an intellectual interest in their lives. They
should be encouraged to read. They should be waked
up to the enormous things happening in the world.
Why, the poor things, they don't even know what
style is. And someone should tell them how much
more effective they could be using a touch of rouge.
Of course I realize that that golden colour may be
attractive to some, but just a little powder, perhaps
a little pink.

If I could only tell them, she was saying. If I could
only tell them, for instance, how to organize. That's
the way to effect changes. Organization. I think the
vote would do them good. They could have more
control over their husbands. And of course, when
they demand more from their husbands, the men
will have to work more, will have to satisfy their new
needs. What do they do now, pray tell me, what
do they produce? What do they give their women?
What they need, if you ask me, is a couple of good
stiff lectures on the advantages of organization.
Also, a few popularized talks on the principles of
Jung and Freud. They look to me too satisfied, too
immobile. They need awakening. They look as
though they had had a great deal of — well, something, I don't know what it is. . . .

We were passing the church and old Blas greeted me. There was a baptism going on. We went in. Blas was making the inscription for the new infant in a big thick book. The father, it seems, was not there. The baby, ventured Blas, has no father. The girl mother holding it, smiled. But, said the lady writer, of course this is not really a baptism then, because how can they give the child a name if it has no father. It was hard to explain to her about such customs, but I explained that there was an official baptism for the children of the legally married ones and that for the rest, which included almost all the Little Mexicans, there was what you might call a " semi-official " baptism. It was really just as good, and, for two pesos, the mother received a nice certificate with whatever name she chose to give the child written on it, signed by the priest. And I pointed out the two registry books to her. She did not understand at first when I said that the thicker of the two was the registry of the baptism of those *without fathers*. Why, she said, a large part of the town must be of illegitimate birth then. It may be, I said, but they are really nice people just the same. They simply accept many little casualties of life here that we make a fuss about. They must. They happen to be affectionate, and they love children. Of course, if a girl is too careless about such things, her neighbours make fun of her. But it is all in good humour.

Oh, said the lady writer. She murmured something about having hoped to be able to write at least one article for the Sunday Magazine about the rise of the New Woman in Mexico. Or it sounded like that.

In the thick book will be found inscribed the name
of one Lola Redondita as a mother. It is in that one
three times and it is also in the book-of-children-
with-fathers once. In the registration of the birth
of her newest infant she states her age as twenty.
That was barely a month ago. She looks eighteen.

Lola herself is a slender, brown little thing, with
very black eyes and fine level black eyebrows. Her
rebozo is the colour of turkey feathers, woven in a
fine, monotonous pattern. Her dresses are all alike,
not very Indian, but some are brighter than others.
One of them is red, and she is a little self-conscious
about it. Others are made over from her mother's
things and she has some shirts that are symphonies
in old-fashioned patterns of grey and black flannel
with tiny flowers, also in character with the turkey-
hen tone.

When she is in the market buying she bargains so
quietly and firmly that no one notices her insistence.
At times, if the price of chiles is very definitely at
four centavos the *cuartillo,* she can entreat with such
charm that they usually let her have them at three. I
have even seen her in such a case go so far as to lay
her hand on the merchant's arm — a most forward
thing for Lola to do — and call the man *Señorito
Chulo!* (charming young sir).

When Lola was fourteen, times were very hard
and her aunt made little objection when a soldier, a
corporal, took her along with him to Iguala. She
came back six months later and had her first child

She has hated the army ever since. She has always had friends. There was young Simeón Ortega, the son of the best mason in town. But Simeón did not marry her. They still live near each other, and Lola, as she herself says, has her little Roberto as a souvenir of Simeón. Simeón, she says, is gente decente. He actually presented her with ten pesos when Roberto was born, which was more than the *pinche soldado* did. That was sweet of Simeón, because it came at a time when corn and work were very scarce in town. Lola tells me that in those days, not even very long ago, she and her two children and her old aunt, with whom they all still live in a single room, had exactly three tortillas a day among them. Her children lived on thin soup and half a tortilla a day apiece. They show it.

Lola's mother lived about the same life as Lola lives today. She was from the coast, where it is much hotter and people wear fewer clothes. Here, she used to long for her country and complain of the cold. She would tell Lola how beautiful it was there. Of the tall alleys of coco palms and the clear, clear rivers running down into the sea. And of the sugar plantations running back as far as one could see toward the tall blue mountains of the cold country. She used to tell Lola of how she always had good clean water for washing, of how she would simply plant two poles, with a few branches on top, in the middle of the broad sandy river, and would work there in the shade all morning, washing, nude except for a cloth about her waist and her rebozo folded on top of her head. Working thus, with a good black *costeño* cigar to puff on, must have been fine. Lola's mother, at least, could not forget it. And she always talked of how handsome the people were there. She came to this town to live because Don Rinaldo, the arriero, brought her, and she loved him very much.

But the cool of the mountains never suited the old lady. What with poverty and heartache for her beloved coast she finally died. Lola was very small. That was during the revolution.

Lola, incidentally, has her father here in the town. But she rarely sees him. When she does, and if he happens to have been drinking, he pats her hand and gives her a half-peso piece. He can well afford to, being one of the best carpenters in a town that is famous for its carpenters.

Lola had been in service to the Doña Petra for a long time after her affair with Simeón Ortega, when a young truck driver from Iguala persuaded her to go to Mexico with him. She left her two children with her aunt and went, taking all her meagre savings. The boy told her he had rich relatives in the capital, so they spent the savings on a good time. He was going to marry her. But at the end of three brief days they had not yet discovered the relatives, and Lola's money had all been spent on movies and on food at the Flor-de-México. The next day the boy left her before daylight. She woke up alone and with the rent of the room to pay. She had a hard time, but finally found a job as a kitchen helper and worked until she had enough money to come home. Then she told Doña Petra her husband had died of pneumonia and the Doña Petra was sorry for her and let her come back to work, until she became " embarrassed." The child that was baptized and registered in the book-of-children-with-fathers bears the name of the boy who took Lola to Mexico. Luckily he has never shown up again.

About two years ago Lola came to work for me. It was difficult to persuade her, because she is very proper, entirely conventional within her ideals. She said, but señor, what will people think if I enter the house of a single sir, and then too, you are one from outside this country and I may not be able to please you with my cooking. Foreigners, they say, are not accustomed to eat strange dishes. Señor, is it true that the Americanos do not eat *mole?* I have also heard that they do not drink water except from bottles. . . . .

It was very difficult. But she finally appeared and all went well. She was quiet and efficient and knew how to make excellent *mole poblano,* and a dessert from common frijoles that was like fine paste of almonds and nuts. Her omelettes filled with *guacamole* of alligator pear and her soup of lentils with six or seven fruits rarely fail to please my friends. Housework is done soundlessly and with incredible economy. Lola is not talkative, but now and then she tells me about life at Doña Petra's and about witches and about how the devil used to come by her house and knock on the door every night at twelve o'clock after she had come back from Mexico. She says there is an old lady who lives just below her house who, when the moon is full, changes herself into a wild boar and wanders about the streets frightening people; some say she eats little children. Lola is very serious about it.

Once I outlined a devil mask with charcoal on the white-washed wall over the kitchen brasero. It could have been easily dusted off, but instead, Lola carefully spread a paper over it, pinning it at the corners. When I lifted a corner and let one eye of the figure show, Lola would turn her back and shudder, so I cleaned it off. But Lola said the devil would certainly revenge himself on her.

And now it seems that he has. For Lola has had another child. About ten months ago I let her visit the coast where her mother's people are. She had always been anxious to go and since I was going to be away, I gave her ten pesos and sent her. In this country, the next village over the hill is another world and though the coast is only six hours away, Lola and her mother had always thought of it as somewhere toward South America. She was delighted. She would bring some conch shells for bordering the garden and, Ay, señor, she said, if my money holds out, I hope to bring back some cocos, too!

Well, it must have been as her mother had always told her. The coast land is not only very beautiful. There are handsome people there, too. Now she has this new child, and it looks like those people from the Pacific. It has clear olive skin and very black eyes, slightly slanted, like the Polynesians, with long lashes, and it laughs all day.

Of course, she said at first that it was a dishonour to my house and that she knew she must leave. She had given absolutely no notice of the coming event, and as a matter of fact was working in the garden when the infant arrived. It meant a bad case of conscience for her, but happily, it did not last long. She had much " *vergüenza,*" as she said — much shame — at first. Señor, I should ask your pardon, because it happened in the house and the house is yours. Therefore, I should ask pardon of you as of my father. When I assured her, with some embarrassment, of my forgiveness, she brightened a little. Ay, señor, she said, they say that woman is a fragile thing. Well, one evening he came in the moonlight and he caught hold of me, and he said that nothing would happen. And then, at that moment, the fragility came over me.

Lotería — something the coloniales do not approve of. The girl on the right side of the Maestro dealing cards is a soldadera. She is from God-knows-where and all they know about her here is, that she was brought to town by a soldier in the detachment for the plaza. The two men on her other side are farmers — you can tell by their exaggeratedly guarded manner of playing; the two women who follow are owners of the little eating-place called The Struggle. Then there is Don Bruno, the tailor, Albino, the charcoal man, then the Arab who has a dry-goods shop on the Plaza Borda, and the little Indian on this side is the municipal president. If it were not for him, perhaps the coloniales would have their way and this childish and absorbing sort of gambling

would be prohibited. These are the people who most enjoy the carpas, *those little wandering street shows where they dance the* rumba, *and have the marionettes for which Mexico will yet be famous abroad. The coloniales still think of themselves as being in the times of Díaz, when all such vulgar manifestations of Indians were " controlled." Don Artemio, the apothecary, says it looks bad, that it wouldn't be so bad, if they played inside a house and used one of those French roulette wheels or something decent. But they play it in these battered tents, and they use dirty cards and these grotesque painted boards and they play it with grains of* corn. *Imagine! A foreigner coming along would think Mexico was still primitive, he says.*

But these friends sitting around the big table have their own ideas about the coloniales. They smile at them. The fact that the little group of apothecaries represents all the concentrated capital of the town bothers them little and they laugh at them for hoarding. They only become a little angry when they have to pay fifty centavos for a purge that is worth about five. The little group of old men gather outside Don Artemio's Pharmacy and talk about new local restrictions, or of how to make the town more colonial. These fellows, the loteria addicts, playing there just across the street, hardly waste a glance on them. The little doctors gossip and they also have their pleasure in showing outsiders the town. But these people do not even mind if tourists never come. They are a little like the people from Tlamacuzapa, who live well but who wear their most tattered clothes when they come in to the plaza here so that these coloniales will not think they are rich and can pay taxes. But the point is that the coloniales live in the past — that these less pretentious ones represent actual Mexico.

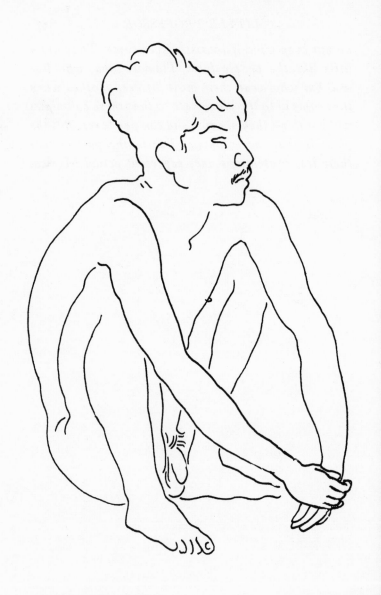

LITTLE PROFESSOR

DON GALINDO Crescencio Gonzales y Gonzaga has little of the traditional professor about him. In fact, you would never know he was a schoolmaster except, perhaps, for the umbrella which he invariably carries. He wears that honourable implement for the sun as well as for the rain, and, I suspect, probably for the dignity which it imparts. Certainly he does not carry it merely because they are being used this year.

Don Galindo is very young. He is young and small and dark. Before he became a maestro he was a silversmith in Iguala. He still treasures the tools of his trade and every now and then he can be found at work in the shade of his small patio fashioning a tiny

189

pair of gold earrings for his baby girl or making his wife a collar of silver beads the size of marbles.

His hands are very brown and quite small, with slender, sensitive fingers, hairless and as smooth as those of his own baby. They are beautiful hands, not unusual for Mexico, and indicate a very different sort of man from the gentleman from Winesburg, Ohio, who had a story written about him. Because this one is not only quiet, but has decision. Though he is a man of ideas, he is not talkative. Except, that is, if one can get him on the subject of agrarianism or rural education — the two things he has had greatest need of and, according to him, the only two great benefits of the Revolution. He is extremely polite and unassuming. Probably that is why he is a professor and not a político. Coming up with the Revolution, he could easily have eventually had a little judgeship or been a tax collector. But somehow he has always been more interested in teaching. Not that he passes the Revolution by. When talking about it, he becomes quite excited, but not in the manner of Don Jesús Llorado. He talks about his race, and there is neither self-conscious pretentiousness nor defensiveness about what he says. He insists that the hope of Mexico lies in the Indian, not in the Whites, that their viewpoint must first be accepted, before it is improved on. You can tell he means it when you have seen him teaching the alphabet to twenty-five little brown disciples.

Unlike Don Jesús and the average mestizo, Don Galindo likes the Americanos. He says they are *cumplidos* — that they are men of their word and that above all they educate their people. Of course, he has no conception of danger to his country in the growing admiration of the Indian for foreign goods and foreign efficiency. He himself wants a radio with six tubes. He also says that the coloniales are short-sighted in opposing the teaching of English, that he personally is most anxious to learn to speak it and he asks if I cannot give him lessons. I will, with much pleasure. Perhaps when he has learned to read with sufficient fluency, I shall lend him Mr. Chase's book on Mexico. It should interest him and perhaps will shock him that anyone should be so frank about his country.

Galindo Gonzales' home is in Iguala, but he was born in a little place called Palo Negro, in the same valley and toward Teloloapan, which accounts for the racial purity of his Iguala profile. Just a few years ago he was still at home and all uneducated. Shortly after the revolution, he remembers the enthusiasm with which his village received the first rural teachers sent out by the new federal ministry of education. He himself was profoundly impressed. He saw vast possibilities opening up for his people in the spread of knowledge and the repartition of lands. He has carried those two ideas with him ever since. In spite of the fact that his father and his father's father had been silversmiths and the fact that he was dedicated to that craft, he was never able to leave off thinking of what he would like to do if he could have an education. That came much later, after the family had moved to Iguala.

Meanwhile, Galindo, with his ideas and his sincerity, had completely captured the confidence of the people of the Palo Negro. In spite of being very young and not even schooled in the art of writing and of making sums, they made him head of their little town. He was named *comisario*.

It is a comparatively rich corner of the valley where Palo Negro is located, one of those small parcels of communal lands that are owned and worked by the village for its own needs, like a single family. The new agrarianism had found immediate root there, the idea of the *ejido,* or communal lands, having existed for centuries among them, before Díaz came along and took away their rights.

The lands had been but recently returned to the people when Galindo became comisario. They say he was zealous, very serious, and very just. His people liked him. There is still a certain anecdote about him that they tell.

It seems that one morning two men in city clothes, with gold watch chains and Texas hats and riding quirts with silver handles rode out to Palo Negro from Iguala. They had an engineer and his assistant with them and without a word they proceeded to survey the lands around the village. Any one could tell at a glance that they were politicians. They had that look. Galindo could see them from the doorway of his little palm-thatched house. It was only distinguished from the dozen houses of his neighbours by a small sign in sober black and white which said *PRESIDENCIA MUNICIPAL.* He saw them there in the next field and he sent two men to tell them they must come to his municipal office and state their business. The men in the Stetson hats told Galindo's emissaries not to bother them. So then Galindo sent four men with rifles, and they told them that it was an order from the Municipal President and they would have to obey. At which the two big men became very angry. They seized the speaker by his white blouse and told him they were deputies from the congress of the nation and that it was in the law that no one in the republic had jurisdiction over what they did and to go back and tell the president to mind his own business or they would make trouble for him.

So Galindo sent his men again, this time with their 30–30 rifles cocked ready in their hands, and the one at their head said to the deputies that he guessed that balls would penetrate deputies as well as anyone else and that they would do them the favour to pass in that moment to the Presidencia Municipal. They went. .

They fumed and they swore and they declared that it was an outrage and they would have Galindo destituted the next day. So Galindo said very well, would they like to draw up the act of accusation right then and there? He would be glad to give them paper and ink and perhaps it could be witnessed and signed that very day. So they did, and one of them — they had not even taken off their Stetsons — sat down and wrote out the act. He wrote it very carefully and very completely and it took nearly an hour. Then he handed it to Galindo where he sat at the other side of the table. Galindo put on spectacles and looked at it for a long time, turning the pages with apparent absorption. He looked very thoughtful while he was at it and it lasted fully forty-five minutes. He finally laid the paper down — then they noticed that he had had it upside down — and he took off his glasses and he said to them very simply: Since I neither know how to read nor to write and since I don't know what it means to be a deputy — if you don't get out of Palo Negro within five minutes I intend to have these men take you out and perforate you and the buzzards and pigs of Palo Negro can finish you. Clear out!

It was not difficult to see that this little brown Galindo meant business. In fact, he has that reputation to this day, even in the quiet of his schoolroom.

The governor eventually heard about the affair of the land-grabbers and, being a good agrarista himself, when the opportunity came, he gave Galindo a scholarship to study in the state normal school at Chilapa. When he was finally sent out on circuit to teach in the mountainous region around Tlapa, he actually came to have more influence than the priests. He persuaded six villages to build community schoolhouses. Five of those, naturally, were named after the governor. The sixth he named for Moises Saenz, the man who had brought rural education to Palo Negro.

The school is in a wing of the old convent. You enter through two patios with white arches and there are masses of purple and red and green bugambilia drenched in sunlight, the quiet permeated with the drone of small voices within. If you are received with any formality, it means that all the little barefoot ones stand up when you enter. The professor comes forward and bows, and when you leave, the children all come forward to kiss the back of your hand and wish that you may go with God. But one of those receptions being enough, I told Don Galindo I would just come and make some sketches and that it would be much better if they would simply forget that I was there.

He is always glad to see me. And on Saturday mornings, if the sun is good and hot, I go by and get him and we go down to the pool in the deep barranca below the Peak of the Cross. It is nice, because several friends, mostly Indians, have found that we do that regularly and we are always joined on the way by others and by the time we arrive at the river it is a good crowd.

Lying there on the smooth round rocks in the hot sun after a plunge in the clear depths, we talk of

many things. He asks if everyone in my country is as pale as I am, and I tell him, much paler. His own body is the colour of a clear Havana cigar, only much smoother, darkening to chocolate on his very flat belly and on his neck. He feels apologetic about it and I tell him he should be proud of his colour, that aesthetically it is a vast advantage which his race has over ours and that Mexico will be fortunate indeed so long as its colour remains as pure as his own. This seems to impress him very much.

His mind is a rich background of legend and local beliefs, and he likes to talk about the different ferns and orchids that depend from the cliff over our heads. He is delighted to find that I also like plants and to be able to tell me about such things as we find in the mountains, and their properties. I note that for almost all of them the name here is in pure Aztec. Even the fruits.

We climb the cascade above the pool. Some of the boys are soaping themselves again and again and washing off in the torrent below. One has a harmonica and sits solitary on a rock, improvising variously on the tune of the Cucaracha.

The little professor is telling me that there was a man who told him once that the Mexicans were descended from the Egyptians, that as proof of it they had built the pyramids at Teotihuacan. And then, too, that he had seen in the paper where Professor Caso held that all the civilization of this side of the Republic had been imported from Indo-China, but that he did not see how that could be, with the Pacific so wide; that neither did he believe in the stories they told about the Aztec language being like the Japanese or like the Greek. And then we both agreed that although it may be theoretically interesting to trace these five thousand year old influences, yet, for those who have a feeling for this country, Mexico is Mexico and, in itself, sufficiently special, sufficiently intense not to need further justification of remote connections.

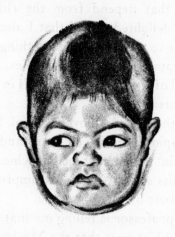